In The Mood

In The Mood

How to Create
Romance, Passion and
Sexual Excitement
By Falling In Love
All Over Again

Doreen Virtue, Ph.D.

National
Press

B O O K S

Library of Congress Cataloging-in-Publication Data

Virtue, Doreen, 1958-
In the mood:
how to create romance, passion and sexual excitement
by falling in love all over again / Doreen Virtue.
256 pp., 15 x 23 cm.
Includes bibliographical references.
ISBN 1-882605-11-X : $19.95
1. Sex—Handbooks, manuals, etc.
2. Sex (Psychology)—Handbooks, manuals, etc.
I. Title.
HQ31.V676   1994
306.7—dc20
93-51490
CIP

*Illustrations on pages 17, 67, 101, 119, 137, 145, 165, 203, 225 and 243
by Charles Dana Gibson*

PRINTED IN THE UNITED STATES OF AMERICA

10   9   8   7   6   5   4   3   2   1

To Michael Tienhaara,
with love and appreciation

Acknowledgments

My sincere gratitude to Joel Joseph, the personable publisher of National Press Books, who took so much time discussing his visions for this book. I also wish to thank Alan Sultan and Shawn Ortiz for organizing the book's publication and publicity, and Talia Greenberg for its editing and design.

I would also like to thank the men and women who allowed me to interview them about their romantic and sexual experiences. These are, of course, very personal topics and I appreciate how much trust went into publicly discussing these issues. Thanks, also, to Chapman University's social science department and the University of California, Irvine medical library for helping me conduct research and student surveys.

And thank you, Joan and Bill Hannan, for your incredible support. You're the best!

Contents

Part II: Recapturing Love's First Blush

Foreword

Were you, like me, raised on romantic fairy tales of princes and princesses who fall in love and live happily ever after? Have you wondered when you'll feel the romantic bliss described in these stories? Do you sometimes feel cheated out of the romance you desire in your relationships? If so, this book is for you.

I have always been interested in love, relationships, passion, and sex. A self-confessed "hopeless romantic," I've always sought romance in my life. Because of this quest, I've experienced some romantic moments that would make great movies or novels. I've had fantastic experiences that I'll always treasure. And as a psychotherapist who has studied the human desire for love, I've become convinced that, for those who want to, it *is* possible to keep passion alive in long-term relationships.

My parents, for example, recently celebrated their 40th wedding anniversary. Mom and Dad have never hidden their romantic attraction to each other. To this day, they often passionately kiss. Many times, the kiss is a spontaneous act occurring as they pass each other in the living room or set the table in the kitchen. My parents taught me that love and romance can occur against such ordinary backdrops. Passion doesn't have to be postponed for an annual vacation, they showed me. Romance need not only occur in a hotel or in an expensive restaurant.

I believe that one partner in a marriage can single-handedly start the romance ball rolling. When one behaves romantically, the fire usually ignites in the other. It has happened time and time again.

Of course, there is important information you need to know before embarking on reinfusing passion into your relationship. The research I conducted in writing this book convinced me, more than ever, of tremendous differences in how men and women view romance. The first thing I learned is that romance is just as, or more, important to men as it is to women. I'm not talking about intercourse. I'm talking about candlelights and soft music. *Both* sexes crave love, tenderness, and romance.

But men and women want romance conveyed in very different ways. And understanding these differences is the key to success in relationships. This book outlines the important distinctions between expressing love to a man and expressing love to a woman. You need this information to communicate romantic love to your partner. This book will help you speak the opposite sex's "romantic language" successfully.

I've also written about how the foods we eat, particularly at dinner, influence romantic feelings. This is a topic I researched and wrote about in two previous books, *The Yo-Yo Syndrome Diet* and *The Chocoholic's Dream Diet*. I later appeared on several talk shows, including "Donahue," "Geraldo," and "Sally Jessy Raphael," discussing how chocolate desserts and high-tryptophan meals determine sexual arousal. Writing this book gave me a valuable opportunity to explore this important topic. Using findings from new studies on brain and food chemistry and how they interact either to enhance or to inhibit sexual arousal, I've included delicious dinner and dessert recipes guaranteed to result in compliments and amour.

Bon Appetit!

—Doreen Virtue
Newport Beach, California

Part I

Unlocking Passion, Releasing Romance

Chapter One
The Passion Drive

"I enjoy a tender, soft look accompanied by a touch that says, 'I love you unconditionally.' It's warm and it shows me his defenses are down. A soft kiss really melts me. I guess the best is an emotional caress and a look reserved just for me."   —37-year-old married woman

"I love it when she puts her arms around me and gives me a big warm smile that says, 'I want you.'"
                              —45-year-old married man

Patricia, a 37-year-old mother of three, complained to her therapist that her husband of nine years, Brian, was not romantic. "He wants to *have sex,* but I want to *make love,*" she sighed. "When we were first together, we'd kiss passionately and spend hours making love and holding each other. Brian used to make me feel so special, so turned on. Now, he expects me to spread my legs whenever he's in the mood. And the worst part is, when we're having sex, I feel he doesn't notice I'm turned off. It's like his body's there, but his mind is a million miles away!"

Brian, sitting next to her in the therapist's office, rolled his eyes skyward. "What does she expect when she never gives me any reason to be turned on? I ask her for oral sex, and she ignores me. If I run my hands over her body, she pushes me away. And on the occasional blue moon when she does agree to have sex, she says, 'Be quiet! You'll wake up the kids!' "

Brian and Patricia were blaming each other for the lack of sexual excitement in their marriage. Their dissatisfactions and their differing beliefs about sex made it impossible for sexual pleasure—except the mechanical, physical sort—to occur. Patricia felt her love life lacked romance; Brian felt blamed for letting her down. Neither partner was experiencing the deep, soul-satisfying sex that they once had shared.

As is the case with many couples, Brian and Patricia needed to get back *in the mood.* Instead of blaming, manipulating, and pressuring each other for sexual and emotional satisfaction, they needed to learn, once again, how to arouse passion and romance, and how to enjoy new levels of sexual ecstasy that would bring them closer together.

This is a book for men and women who, like Brian and Patricia, want more romantic and sexual excitement in their relationships and marriages. Based on 10 years of clinical and non-clinical research with thousands of people, this book provides you with step-by-step guidelines for breathing life into relationships that have gone stale.

If you are a woman, you will learn sure-fire steps to inspire romance in your man. You will also read why manipulating or pressuring men for romance never works and usually backfires. The book also discusses how to create an atmosphere favorable to passion, and suggests sexual positions designed to enhance pleasure for both partners.

If you are a man, you'll appreciate the book's discussion of women's sexual and romantic desires. You'll learn how to share in her fantasies for mutual pleasure and enjoyment, and how she'll express gratitude in ways you never dreamed possible! You will read why simply buying her roses and champagne—even if she asks for them—isn't the key to unlocking her true passions.

Men and women will read little-known ways to experience deeply satisfying *romantic* sex, including step-by-step instructions. You'll learn ways to relax and to have fun with each other, and why this fun leads to spontaneous, satisfying passion.

We All Want the Same Thing

Deep down, men and women share common desires for love, acceptance, and sexual satisfaction. I conducted a survey, asking men and women between the ages of 18 and 70, "On a scale of one to 10, with 10 being the highest, how important is romance to you?" Forty-two percent of the men answered "nine or 10," as did 35 percent of the women. And fully 75 percent of the men surveyed gave romance a rating of seven or above. Eighty-one percent of the women said that romance was seven, eight, nine or 10 on the scale of importance. The results are clear: *Both* sexes care deeply about romance.

In response to this question, many people asked me: "What do you mean by romance?" I responded in turn:

"What do *you* mean by romance?" What I learned is how diverse people's definitions are for "romance." Of course, there is no right or wrong answer, because everyone is different.

There are *major* differences between men's and women's romantic and sexual desires. Understanding these differences enhances the love life, because it is so enjoyable to be with a partner who is pleased or sexually aroused. When both partners receive pleasure, the relationship remains alive and exciting.

In the chapters that follow, you'll read the essential components that both men and women desire in their love and sex lives. Though your life's experiences may have already taught you a lot about the opposite sex, continuing education about sex, romance, and passion can arouse new skills and interests in you. By incorporating this carnal knowledge into your sexual repertoire, your sexual experiences stay fresh and exploratory instead of mechanical and routine.

Your Sexual Self

Before we look at the opposite sex, there's one important consideration: *you.* The truth is, you can have the most exciting, physically attractive sexual partner in the world—but unless you're mentally prepared for passion, you won't enjoy the full experience of ecstasy. This is what I call your "Sexual Self." This means being excited about your life, feeling turned-on and aroused by life and enjoying your own company and those around you. It means, literally, *flirting with life.*

Let me further explain by asking you a few personal questions. You may either write down your responses or answer them in your head:

♥ Question 1: On a scale of one to 10, with 10 being highest, how important is romance to you?

♥ Question 2: When I ask what romance means to you, what's the first thought that enters your mind?

♥ Question 3: When was the last time you felt strong feelings of passion, romance, or sexual arousal?

♥ Question 4: What factors influenced those feelings? Think of all possible components, including the people around you, the time of day, how you were feeling physically, mentally and emotionally, what music, movie or reading material may have been involved, and what you ate or drank immediately before the feeling occurred.

♥ Question 5: Please complete the following sentence: "My love life would be much better, if only: _____ ."

Your answers to these questions underscore just how much passion and romance begin with *you*, and how little these emotions have to do with other people. While we all respond to outside stimulation—attractive people, sexy movies or magazines, certain foods or drinks—our arousal comes from how we feel or think about this outside stimulation.

For example, Barbara answered Question 5: "... if only I could lose my extra weight." Ted answered the same question with: "... if only my wife would wear lingerie and behave more seductively." And Annette said: "... if only I could meet a man who wasn't afraid of commitment."

All three believed that their love lives hinged on outside factors such as lingerie, weight, or choice of sexual partners. And these factors do influence our passions significantly. However, before we can really enjoy sex, passion and romance, we must be aroused with our own lives. Barbara can lose all the weight she wants, but until she's truly happy with herself, she'll continue to feel romantically disappointed. Ted's wife could become a *Victoria's Secret* centerfold, but unless he feels sexier about himself, he'll only find something else to complain about. The same applies to Annette, who could receive a marriage proposal from Mr. Right tomorrow, and turn it down because something inside her is still not quite right.

Recharging Your Sexual Self

You don't need to go through elaborate introspection to breathe life into your sexual self. One of the easiest ways to add zest and sexual energy to your life is to recapture the ability to flirt with life. Do you recall a morning when you woke up excited about the day, when you felt especially good about who you were? Maybe you were newly in love; or maybe you felt good about how you looked, or were anticipating a special event. This is the feeling of a charged sexual self, based on the sexual energy we all have within us.

We don't need to wait for, or rely upon, outside circumstances to create these feelings. We can do it ourselves. If you think about how you feel and act when you're newly in love, you'll recall that the world takes on brighter colors, that everything seems pleasurable, and that you like everyone just a little bit more than usual.

You can capture that newly-in-love feeling no matter what your relationship status, by focusing on the world as though you *were* newly in love. In other words, make yourself notice the leaves, clouds, birds, and sky as you drive or walk to work. Smile and say "hello" to people. Spend time talking to people you encounter—the newsstand attendant, the gas station cashier, the office mail clerk. Enjoy your interactions with strangers—don't just rush through them. You'll find that your mood—and theirs—will brighten with shared jokes, warm smiles, and even flirtatious glances.

Take the risk to look others in the eyes and to smile. I'm not talking about inappropriate or potentially dangerous times such as when you're walking down a desolate street late at night. But, when you're grocery shopping, what's wrong with making a comment about the produce to whomever may be standing next to you? You'll find that by innocently flirting with people—both of the same and opposite sexes—your energy will be lifted and infused with good feelings. These are the same emotions that accompany new love, and that charge your sexual self.

Try it today. The next time you encounter someone, look in their eyes until you catch their glance for two or three seconds. It may feel a little awkward, but fix on their eyes and smile. Your mouth or your eyes can say, "Hello." Then see what follows. The worst that can happen is that they'll ignore you or seem uncomfortable or embarrassed; the best is that they'll return your smile or "hello," and maybe even share a short conversation or a joke with you. You may make a new friend!

But remember, this isn't flirting as we think about it in the conventional, sexual sense. This is flirting with life, and that's why I'm advocating eye contact and interactions with other people, whatever their physical attractiveness, age, or gender. This is flirting solely for the burst of energy and enjoyment that it creates.

Satisfied In Bed, Satisfied In Life

If you're bored with your love life, if sex seems routine, and passion and romance are abstract concepts, chances are you're also bored with other areas of your life. I hear these complaints all the time. Women say, "My husband's so unromantic!" Men claim, "I want a woman who knows how to make a man happy."

Legitimate complaints? Of course. But will they ever get resolved? Here's what I've learned by talking with and counseling thousands of men and women over the years:

1. You can inspire romance and passion in your partner. Donna was a 43-year-old schoolteacher who felt that her marriage had gone stale, bereft of any romance. Donna blamed her husband for the malaise in their marriage: "It's like that song says, 'You don't bring me flowers anymore.' When we were dating and when we first got married, Brian couldn't stop kissing me. Now, I'm lucky if I get a peck on the cheek."

Donna's husband had changed, she complained. But was *he* the only one who had changed? I asked Donna to recall how she had acted during their courtship. During dating, she recalled, she'd dress up, pay close attention to Brian's words, laugh at his jokes and cook him sumptuous dinners. Donna learned that if she wanted a Prince Charming, she'd have to be more of a Fairy Tale Princess herself. It's like anything in life: You reap what you sow. If you want your husband to be more of a gentleman, you need to be more of a lady. And vice versa.

♥ But I don't have time!

♥ I don't want to have to dress up for my husband!

♥ I want to relax when I get home!

These are all legitimate concerns. But you can infuse passion into your relationship by making small efforts to be thoughtful. Little things like looking at your partner when he or she is talking. Keeping your body and breath pleasant-smelling. Giving your partner a romantic or sexy card.

Remember, you can't control your partner's actions; you can only control your own. So why not concentrate on being the best romantic partner you can be, and feel pleased when your spouse responds with renewed passion and sexual energy?

2. People who are happy with their lives are more sexually satisfied and sexually appealing. A study on what attracts us to other people made an interesting conclusion. It stated that everyone—both men and women—is consistently attracted to relaxed and confident people. If you think about your own tastes in people, you'll probably find that this is true for you, too. Sure, we all have height, weight, and hair-color preferences when looking at others. But the personality style we find most attractive usually fits the "relaxed and confident" model.

Both terms are important. People who are confident, but not relaxed, often make poor first impressions. They can appear boastful and boorish. Or they may seem anxious and uptight. People who are relaxed, but not confident, may seem to have low self-esteem, leading others to wonder, "What's wrong with that person?" Think about movie stars or people on television whom you admire (or about whom you have romantic or sexual fantasies). Aren't they confident and relaxed? This demeanor comes from feeling happy and satisfied with life—with making, striving for, and achieving goals.

My client Linda is a perfect example. She came to me after reading my book *The Yo-Yo Syndrome Diet*. Linda was lonely and wanted to be in love and married; and she was convinced that she needed to lose 75 pounds in order to achieve this goal. Linda was one of those people who is always told, "You have such a pretty face! If only you'd lose some weight, you'd be beautiful!"

But Linda needed to do more than simply lose the weight. She needed to recapture the love of herself. In fact, I told Linda that she probably wouldn't lose much weight until she increased her self-esteem. This is because it takes a great deal of self-confidence to achieve a goal as ambitious as losing 75 pounds. We worked on her self-esteem and weight simultaneously.

Linda used affirmations, such as those outlined later in this book, to begin feeling better about herself. She also began taking better care of herself physically by doing important little things: replacing her torn, old bras and panties; getting a long-put-off physical exam; having a manicure and a pedicure. In doing all these things, Linda began to feel *really* good about herself as a person. She didn't need to eat all the time to feel good, so she began to lose weight.

About a month after she began therapy, Linda's weight was down by 10 pounds. She was still a very large person, but she was looking more beautiful, radiating with a glow of happiness and self-assurance. Linda dressed better, smiled bigger, and stood taller than she had for years.

She was asked to join two normal-weight female friends at a dance the following weekend. At one time, Linda would have avoided a social situation so fraught with potential rejection; but she was feeling good about herself, so she donned her prettiest outfit, and joined her friends. And guess what happened? Linda was asked to dance practically every dance!

I wish I could have been there to see her at that dance. Knowing Linda, she probably had her raven hair twisted up in a pretty chignon. Her red lips were probably in a constant smile. And her large, doe-like eyes were probably making contact with everyone in the room. Linda didn't need to postpone love until she lost weight; she simply needed to be happy with herself in order to inspire happiness in others.

Things To Do To Make Yourself Feel Sexy

Do you consider yourself a sexy person? Everyone is sexy deep down, because all humans are sexual beings.

You don't need to be a Tom Cruise or Michelle Pfeiffer look-alike to be sexy, as we've learned.

Here are some ways to perk up your sexual self:

For Women

♥ Wear a push-up, padded bra and a plunging neckline blouse or a tight sweater (no matter how old you are, this is guaranteed to make you feel giddy with sexual appeal).

♥ Paint your fingernails and lips a sultry shade of red.

♥ Buy a cotton, thong-style body suit from the lingerie or exercise-wear department. Whether you wear it with pants, a skirt, or to your aerobics class, the thong is really very comfortable (more comfortable than it looks) and will make you feel sinfully sexy!

♥ Wear thigh-high hose and garters under your business suit. Only you will know why your spirits are extra high!

♥ Reshape your eyebrows using tweezers, cosmetic scissors (not as painful as it sounds), and an eyebrow pencil.

♥ Wear false eyelashes. Even the small "demi-whisper" variety will accentuate your eyes and make you feel like batting your lashes and flirting!

For Men

♥ Take a bright red, too-expensive sports car out for a test drive and pretend you're ready to buy it.

♥ Buy and wear a silk necktie with unusual colors, such as sea-foam green, sky blue, or any variety of pinks, magentas, and purples. You'll be amazed at the compliments you'll get from women and men!

♥ Splash on extra aftershave and cologne. Invest in coordinating scents (cologne, deodorant, lotion, etc.) of your favorite fragrance.

♥ Are you still wearing old boxer shorts or baggy BVDs? Try some tight-fitting bikini underwear, and you'll notice how they boost your spirits and make you feel younger!

♥ Splurge on a sexy pair of Porsche Carrera sunglasses. Women love them!

♥ Buy something in silk, for lounging around the house. Silk pajamas or a silk bathrobe can make you feel like the king of the castle that you are.

For Both Sexes

♥ Wear a pair of faded blue jeans—extra tight! Even better, tear a hole in them dangerously close to a sexy spot on your body.

♥ Get an all-over body massage. This is less expensive than you think, and the results are both immediate and long lasting.

♥ Buy an outfit normally worn by people 10 (or more!) years younger than you.

♥ Rub cologne through your hands and then through your hair when you dress in the morning. Every time you brush or comb your hair during the day, the smell—and your sex appeal—will be revived.

♥ Cover the gray in your hair with a do-it-yourself rinse.

♥ Start a discussion about "favorite sexual fantasies" with your friends.

♥ Rent a sexy movie.

♥ Give yourself the vacation-fresh look of a bronzed tan with one of the new self-tanning creams or sprays. They create quick, natural-looking tans with none of the orange, streaky problems associated with the self-tanners made years ago.

♥ Put satin sheets on the bed. Yes, they're slippery and too hot and sticky during warm weather, but oh are they sexy—and worth it!

Chapter Two
Men and Romance

*"The best things between a man and a woman are unspoken.
Communication through the eyes and touch is ideal. The
fewer amounts of spoken words, the better."*
                                    —*25-year-old unmarried man*

The fact that men and women are different creatures is
accepted by most people. Romance occurs precisely *because* of these differences! The way in which a man and
woman's bodies fit so perfectly together—whether
they're intertwined in an embrace, "spooning" side by

side, or engaged in passionate lovemaking—has always impressed me as a masterpiece of Nature's planning.

Male and female differences may be viewed as complimentary, like two pieces of a puzzle that lock together perfectly—or as problems. "If only men were more expressive," women complain. "If only women were more relaxed," men lament.

Understanding the distinctions between men and women helps us to "connect" romantically with the opposite sex. It helps us to interpret their ways of thinking and to understand why they act in certain ways.

Women often wish men would be "more romantic." What they really mean is, "I wish men were more romantic in the way women are romantic." My conversations, therapy sessions, and surveys of men yielded overwhelming evidence that men are extremely romantic—maybe even more romantic than women.

More men than women said that romance was extremely important to them. Their definitions of romance were, of course, different from women's. But they didn't automatically link romance to sex, as stereotypes about men often suggest. Instead, their feelings and thoughts concerning romance followed a distinctly "male" pattern.

The Visual Male

You may have learned about the different uses for the left and right hemispheres of the brain's cerebral cortex. The left lobes are primarily used for processing words and verbal information. The right side is devoted to abstract reasoning, visual skills, and mathematical problem solving.

In general, women are primarily left-brain dominant and men are right-brain dominant. Men are more likely to be skilled at math, science, and other areas involving abstract reasoning. Women are often more proficient in verbal skills such as writing and communications. Traditional occupations reflect these gender-specific traits, with more men entering science, engineering, and air traffic control than women. And, while women are capable of mastering any field, *traditionally* female-dominated careers reflect a higher verbal ability, such as teaching and journalism.

These brain differences also mean that men's inner worlds are based upon what they *see*, while women organize their thoughts more upon what they *hear*. In other words, men are visual and women are auditory.

What does this mean to romance? For one thing, men are aroused more by what they see than by what they hear. They use visual aids, such as magazines and vivid fantasies, for arousal. For women, words and thoughts are more arousing than pictures.

Women's romantic preferences and fantasies will be discussed further in Chapter Three. For now, let's concentrate on men.

The Look of Love

When I began surveying men about romance, I expected to read many answers that connected sex to love and romance. I was pleasantly surprised to find that the men's answers were much more removed from the act of intercourse than I expected.

What this survey revealed was that men are very romantic people. So why is the opposite stereotype—that men are unromantic and interested only in sex—so firmly held, even by trained professionals such as myself and my colleagues in psychology? For one thing, men's expressions of romance are misunderstood because theirs are typically quieter than those of women. Since men are visual and not auditory, they don't use romantic words to the extent that most women would like and expect. They express romance in more subtle ways, that may go unnoticed, and are often misread.

They also are aroused by non-auditory romantic cues. This means that *words* don't turn men on, but *actions* do. Here's a list of the actions most often cited by men as turn-ons leading to a romantic mood, listed in order from most to least frequent:

♥ Being with a woman who looks good or dresses seductively

♥ A home-cooked dinner

♥ Non-sexual touching, such as hugging, massaging, or caressing

♥ Eye contact or a special way of looking at each other

♥ Low lights or candlelight

♥ Having a partner who makes a special effort to make a romantic evening

♥ Having a partner who is spontaneous or who surprises me

♥ Kissing

♥ Soft music

♥ Wine or champagne

♥ A woman who smells great

♥ A quiet atmosphere.

All these turn-ons strike me as gentle, tender expressions of male and female bonding. A romantic setting is very important to a man—he enjoys dimmed lights, soft music and a quiet atmosphere. His romantic mood is aroused when his female partner puts a special effort into making him feel like a king.

You can read this list and almost conjure up a mental picture of his ideal romantic evening. He comes home from work and is greeted at the door by his wife or his girlfriend, who is dressed in a seductive outfit and is wearing a sexy perfume. The smells of dinner cooking entice him. She wraps her arms around him, and they kiss passionately. She pops the champagne cork and they unwind by snuggling on the couch with their drinks.

Later, they enjoy their dinner at home, with candlelight and soft music piercing the otherwise-quiet room. They look at each other lovingly; she strokes his hand and his thigh. No words are exchanged, but both know that the other is aroused.

This is very similar to the romantic fantasies of women, as you'll read in Chapter Three, with one important distinction—his romantic ideals are unspoken scenarios; hers are filled with verbal expressions.

One of the most surprising results of the survey was the different ways men and women felt about *talking* during romantic moments. Men consistently said that they appreciated nonverbal communication between the sexes, such as a look, a touch, or a smile. Women, on the other hand, overwhelmingly told me they wanted to *hear* that their men loved them. Both sexes need to feel loved and appreciated—they only want it expressed differently.

"Please Just Love Me"

Women want verbal expressions of love, and men prefer nonverbal exchanges, and these differences lead to frustrations. Women, not understanding their men's subtle and quiet expressions of romance, often verbalize their frustrations—and not always in the kindest ways.

A woman may complain to her husband, "You're so unromantic. Why don't you give me cards or tell me you love me?" What she may not understand is that her husband's automatic patterns of thinking about romance—what comes naturally to him—do not include giving cards or expressing romantic words. In other words, these are not natural expressions of romance for a man.

Unfortunately, when a woman complains to her man, it has the opposite effect than the one she desires. Instead of creating romance, her criticisms about his behavior are perceived as criticisms of *him*. And, right or wrong, this is a man's biggest turnoff. Remember, a man is aroused when he feels that his woman appreciates and admires him. He is equally turned off when he feels that his girlfriend or wife disapproves of him.

Here is a list of the most frequent answers men gave to the survey question, **"What spoils a romantic mood for you?"** The responses most frequently mentioned:

- ♥ Arguments

- ♥ Criticisms

- ♥ When a woman talks about, or compares me to past boyfriends or husbands

- ♥ When my partner nags me

- ♥ When my partner complains

- ♥ A woman who is selfish or self-centered

- ♥ A woman who is in a bad mood or who is unhappy

- ♥ A woman who pushes for sex before I'm ready.

Other turnoffs for men went along the same lines. Men got "out of the mood" when they perceived their female partners as insecure, negative, disinterested, or asking too many questions. To me, these female characteristics are probably their way of trying to get the men to be "more romantic." But when a man perceives himself as criticized, pushed, or manipulated, he loses his romantic mood. Then, both partners lose the opportunity to enjoy a beautiful evening together.

Pop star Madonna advises women in one of her hits, "You've got to make him express himself." The song's premise is that a woman should not settle for an unexpressive man, but should "make" him tell her how he feels. The song makes sense on the surface—until you consider how much success the singer has had in her own love life.

Romantically-frustrated women who discard relationship after relationship, believing that Prince Charming is just around the next corner, are missing opportunities in the present. Remember, men are *very* romantic. They want and need affection, love, and passion just as much as women want and need them. Men may need romance in their love relationships even more than women typically do, since men's emotional needs are not met by close friendships as much as women's are.

Women need to "hear" men's romantic expressions with a very finely-tuned ear. The first step is to arouse, or to inspire, romance in both partners. The chapters of this book outline ways to create romantic atmospheres and conditions. Women can remind themselves, by reading the men's romantic "wish list," of ways to arouse romantic feelings in their men. In reading this list, notice how much emphasis men put on women's actions. Man, the visual creature, wants woman to *show* her appreciation and love. Believe me, he'll be inspired to return your affections.

"But I'm too tired to cook dinner when I come home from work!" women tell me. In talking with men, however, I've found that it's the effort that's most appreciated when it comes to romance. You don't have to knock yourself out baking homemade bread with dinner. If your husband or your boyfriend can see that you've tried to create a special evening (remember the candles with dinner!), it endears you to him. It makes him feel loved and special. And that will inspire him to shower you with kisses, hugs, and caresses.

Men's Romantic Language

Like most women, I longed for a romantic relationship with a sincere charmer who would sweep me off my feet with expressions of love. The men I was involved with never satisfied my romantic desires to hear words of appreciation and adoration. I wanted to be put on a pedestal and to be pampered with romance.

I got my wish, and then I was sorry.

He was a handsome French-Canadian, with a romantic French accent and a background in public singing. He swept me off my feet by singing love songs to me in French, and showering me with cards, gifts, and phone calls just to say, "I love you." Here was the expressive man I was looking for.

In fact, he had all the ingredients you could imagine for an ideal romantic partner. Incredibly handsome, he was a cross between Mel Gibson and Mikhail Baryshnikov— really! He was devoted, monogamous, and eager to get married. He was a great cook. He owned his own business, in which he was fairly successful. He spoke fluent French and had a great singing voice.

So what was the problem? Well, this was the most expressive person, let alone man, I had ever met. He talked about his feelings nonstop, to the point where I would sometimes think, "Would you just shut up?" I mean, he never stopped talking! His expressions weren't limited to the positive aspects he loved about me. Oh no! Along with the sweetest compliments I'd ever received, he'd say everything else that was on his mind. He'd tell me what a beautiful face I had, and then inform me that I should apply my makeup a different way or change the color of my hair. In other words, my "dream expressive man" would tell me everything that was in his head and heart, even if I didn't care to hear about it.

I'm no longer with this man, but I did learn an important lesson about men and women while I was with him. I learned to appreciate "normal" men, who are much less expressive about the negative and positive thoughts they have. I also learned to tune in and notice men's subtler, nonverbal expressions of love.

These subtle romantic expressions follow men's beliefs that love should be "seen and not heard." In other words, a man will show his love through his actions. Action, or showing, is a language in which he's fluent. He also assumes that his partner understands this language, and is very surprised when she asks for verbal reassurances of his love.

Examples of How Men Show Love and Caring

♥ Going to work every day

♥ Paying the bills

♥ Being with you or being married to you

♥ Watching television with you

♥ Fixing or washing your car

♥ Fixing or cleaning things around the house

♥ Giving you advice and suggestions on how to solve problems

♥ Providing discipline or guidance for the children

♥ Explaining or teaching something to you

♥ Pulling the chair out from the table for you

♥ Going shopping with you

♥ Taking out the garbage

♥ Mowing the lawn

♥ Giving the dog a bath (so you don't have to)

♥ Holding doors open for you

♥ Hugging, kissing, massaging, or caressing you

♥ Complimenting you (even if it's a brief compliment)

♥ Making love to you

♥ Eating your cooking

♥ Washing and/or drying the dishes

♥ Accompanying you to an event you consider important

♥ Buying gifts

♥ Paying for household items or vacations

♥ Visiting with your friends or relatives

♥ Laughing at your jokes.

Notice how many of these expressions are nonverbal. Many of them are things women consider routine or unromantic, such as "going to work every day" or "paying the bills." But to a man, these are very important expressions of devotion to his wife and family. They are fundamental parts of being a man and a provider. They stem, in fact, from that part of men's natures I call "The Knight."

The Shining Armor of Love

The differences between men and women are based partly on physiological distinctions, and partly on how boys and girls are socialized and raised. From the time they are born, boys are expected to be strong, both physically and emotionally. They hear, "Don't be a sissy! Don't cry like a girl!"—and before they realize the sexism of these words, the messages are deeply ingrained.

Little boys, just like little girls, want to be accepted and appreciated by parents, teachers, and friends. They learn that being strong and tough are the ways to winning acceptance, and these ideals are embedded for a lifetime. The male framework is based on fables of the "knight in shining armor." His ideal self is a conquering hero who saves people—mostly women—in distress.

A man carries this need to be a hero into all situations, to different degrees. In relationships, the lessons learned in early childhood still influence him. He must be stronger and tougher than a girl, or else he's a sissy. Women who understand this need can appreciate and even benefit from it. Women who misinterpret it will run into problems with relationships.

One time the Knight usually appears is when the damsel—his wife or his girlfriend—is in distress. This is his opportunity to be her hero, and to win the love and approval of the damsel, and maybe gain the kingdom as well. But if she's not asking to be rescued, bitter misunderstandings may occur.

For example, Lisa came home from the office upset because a co-worker had taken credit for Lisa's hard work. She wanted a sympathetic ear from her husband, Carl. Lisa simply wanted to vent and to complain. Carl, however, thought she wanted help; so instead of only listening and empathizing, he began offering Lisa suggestions on how to fix the situation.

Lisa would complain about how mean her co-worker was, expecting Carl to shake his head in sympathy or maybe give her a comforting hug. Instead, Carl thought Lisa wanted to be "rescued" with advice on how to confront the co-worker. Lisa felt unheard, as though Carl wasn't listening or sympathizing with her. Carl, on the other hand, felt frustrated, because every suggestion he offered was met with a "Yes, but—" response. Carl couldn't understand why Lisa wasn't accepting his help.

Had Lisa and Carl understood these male and female differences more clearly, the scenario would have been more harmonious. Lisa would have told Carl what she needed—a sympathetic ear—and he would have tried to provide it. Lisa would have acknowledged Carl's advice, and told him how much she appreciated his desire to be helpful, whether she followed his suggestions or not. In other words, each would have spoken in the other's language.

When men offer help, advice, and suggestions, it is usually because they wish to be the hero of the household. Women who keep this in mind will listen graciously, and when appropriate, accept this offer of assistance. This doesn't mean that the woman should act helpless or needy. She also shouldn't be patronizing and pretend to accept his advice if she has no plans of doing so. Men will see through these manipulations and feel resentful.

Both sexes simply need to understand the other person's "language of love." Instead of being irritated by his suggestions, instead of feeling offended that he is criticizing her, a woman should hear her man's advice for what it is: an act of love. He doesn't necessarily think he's better or smarter than she is. He doesn't think she needs improving. He just wants to be her hero. Period.

The Sexual Male

I'll never forget a television interview with a prostitute who said, "If wives would give their husbands oral sex, we hookers would be out of business." It's true. Men love oral sex, and the second part of this book goes into explicit detail on techniques and methods for both partners' maximum pleasure. For now, I'd like to consider how men's sexual preferences fit into their "knight in shining armor" model.

Boys identify with their genitals much more than girls do, because a penis is much more noticeable than a clitoris or a vagina. Boys are aware of their private parts before they even know how to spell their names. They feel proud of their penises, and gain pleasure from the time of their first erection and orgasm in early adolescence.

Boys' emotional ties to their genitals are similar to the way girls feel about their emerging breasts. Both breasts and penises are linked to sexuality, and both are given undue attention during adolescence. There are also many insecurities tied to breasts and penises. Boys and girls wonder if their penises and breasts are big enough, or if they'll keep growing. They compare themselves to classmates in the locker room and in gym showers.

Adolescents commonly experiment with quasi-homosexuality. Boys often engage in "circle jerks," a form of group masturbation. Girls often feel one another's breasts during slumber parties. These practices are common, but many of my patients felt something was wrong with them because they had engaged in them.

As adults, men still carry strong emotions about their penises. In particular, they need nonverbal reassurance from their lovers that their penises are big, or at least adequate and satisfying. One of the ways men feel appreciated is through oral sex. When a woman kisses, licks, and sucks his penis and testicles, a man feels approved of and loved. She is, in essence, kissing the very essence of his manhood when she takes his penis into her mouth. And if she swallows his semen, she is literally "accepting" him into her body.

Oral sex is enormously physically pleasurable for men. But its greatest pleasure stems from its symbolism. Men's locker room talk is often sprinkled with boasts about how their wives or girlfriends "swallow." This may sound crude, but it's essentially the equivalent of mythical knights bragging of the medals they earned for saving the king's palace.

Men, and women, want to know they are approved of and loved. Men just need to "hear" this love and approval in their language of *action*. You can tell your man that you appreciate his lovemaking skills, but be cautious with the words you use. Never, ever sound like you're comparing him to past lovers. Don't say, "You're a much better lover than Tom was," because this will create a picture in your man's mind of you making love to Tom. Remember how visual men are.

It is so much better to show your appreciation than to say it! If you must say something during lovemaking, keep it short and sweet, such as, "You're my king," or, "You're such a great lover." But only say those things if you mean them, because men are sensitive to, and turned off by, insincerity.

Above all, never criticize his penis during an argument. No matter how angry you are, if you ever expect to have a good relationship with your man, you should never say anything negative about his penis size or his sexual skills. Once you say that, he'll neither forget it nor forgive you, and the relationship will never again be the same.

Chapter Three
Women and Romance

"The best thing my fiancé could do to put me in a romantic mood would be if he were to hold me and tell me how he feels about me, and what I mean to him. I love affection and sharing my feelings, and when he does that to me, I feel so good!"   —22-year-old unmarried woman

Repeatedly, the women surveyed for this book told me how much they wanted to hear their men say, "I love you." As women, we tend to be left-brain dominant, and thus tend to be very responsive to words and verbal expressions. You may recall from Chapter Two that men are primarily visual, right-brain dominant people. Men show love (visual); women speak about love (auditory). Men want to *see* that women love them; women want to *hear* that men love them.

No wonder the sexes have such difficulty understanding each other. We speak in completely different languages! It's as though a Russian were trying to teach a Spaniard how to program her VCR. The process of programming a VCR, or having a love relationship, is difficult enough without a language barrier. But, the reality is that men and women think differently—he in pictures, she in words. The first step in overcoming this language barrier is really to try to understand each other.

The survey results conducted for this book revealed a troubling cycle that blocks intimacy, spoils romance, and ruins relationships. It goes like this:

1. The man and woman fall in love.

2. The woman longs to hear the man express his love verbally. Occasionally, he'll remember to say something loving. But since this is not his primary language (showing instead of saying is his way of expressing love), he forgets to say loving words.

3. The woman feels frustrated because he's not whispering sweet words of love or appreciation. She may feel:

♥ **Worried** (*"Maybe he doesn't love me anymore"*)

♥ **Jealous** (*"I'll bet he's attracted to someone else"*)

♥ **Angry** (*"He's taking me for granted and doesn't appreciate all the things I do for him"*)

♥ **Insecure** (*"I wonder if he's planning on leaving me?"*).

4. The woman asks the man, "Do you love me?" The man doesn't understand why she's asking. After all, he *shows* her he loves her through his actions. He doesn't realize that she needs to hear the words.

5. The woman continues to feel upset because she repeatedly has to ask for romantic expressions and proclamations. She acts aggressively or passive-aggressively as a reaction; perhaps she'll try to make the man feel jealous, or maybe pressure him to "show" more love. She tries coaxing, manipulating, complaining, and seducing—anything to alleviate the horrible feeling that "he doesn't love me," or, "he isn't attracted to me anymore." She wants him to say words of love and reassurance. If he doesn't say these things, she panics and feels hurt. And when nothing else works, she complains.

6. The man interprets these actions as signals that the woman doesn't love him, or that she's got a personal problem such as bitchiness, mood swings, or PMS. Men usually attribute women's complaints to a problem she's having, and rarely blame themselves as the instigators of her complaints. Extensive research has repeatedly concluded that blaming outside forces for problems, while taking personal credit for success, is a characteristic of high self-esteem. This doesn't mean that irresponsibility equates high self-regard; it means that not blaming yourself, or not taking responsibility for other people's problems and bad moods, does. People with low self-esteem internalize and reproach themselves for problems around them. Regardless, the more the woman pressures the man, the less he'll react with the response she really wants.

Remember from Chapter Two, men do not like women to complain, to ask many questions, or to show a negative attitude. Unfortunately, women who are frustrated, who feel unloved, often come across as complaining, negative people. Women unknowingly sabotage their own purposes by turning men off with complaints and accusations.

If men understand how important verbal expressions of love are to women, and if women understand how much their actions mean to men, both sexes can avoid misunderstandings. But, just as people conversant in many languages usually revert to their native tongues, especially when they feel tired or stressed, the sexes tend to "forget" to speak the other's language regularly.

When we enter a new love relationship, we often hold the illusion that "this time, things will be different." We look at our new beloved partner, and we feel a special camaraderie, a unique closeness. We project many fantasies about our ideal lover onto this person, and we often believe that the new lover is a lot like ourselves. "We have so much in common," is frequently heard from newly-in-love people. We only look for, and therefore only find, what is positive.

We tend to forget, in the beginning of a love relationship, how differently men and women see the world. Later, after the fog of the relationship's newness begins to lift, we recognize these gender-based differences and mistakenly assume, "This isn't my ideal lover after all. My dream lover thinks exactly as I do." But in male/female relationships, the point is to find compatible differences in viewpoints.

All I Want To Do Is Love You

Once men and women understand the gender-based differences, and how they affect romantic desires, a lot of healing begins. Both sexes become more patient with each other, and they can even learn to laugh at the differences.

We learned in Chapter Two about men's romantic desires, and their nonverbal ways of expressing love. Now, let's look at women's typical romantic preferences.

What Turns Women On

♥ Non-sexual touching (hugging, massage, caressing)

♥ Dinner, especially homemade

♥ The man shows interest in me and in what I have to say

♥ Conversation

♥ The man says, "I love you"

♥ The man compliments me

♥ Low lights or candlelight

♥ Surprises and spontaneity

♥ Kissing

♥ The man makes a special effort in planning the date

♥ Dancing, especially alone at home

♥ The man gives me flowers, especially for no special reason

♥ Soft music

♥ The man doesn't pressure me to have sex

♥ The man gives me a special "look" or eye contact

♥ Going for a walk together

♥ The man gives me a loving note or card

- ♥ Wine, champagne, or other alcohol

- ♥ Sunrises, sunsets, or moonlight

- ♥ Being next to the ocean, a lake, or other water.

What Turns Women Off

- ♥ The man pushes me to have sex

- ♥ Arguments

- ♥ The man smells bad

- ♥ The man is selfish

- ♥ The telephone, noise, or other people interrupt the romantic moment

- ♥ The man has poor manners

- ♥ The man seems insincere

- ♥ The man talks about his previous girlfriends or his ex-wife

- ♥ The man has a negative attitude.

Ladies: Last To Love, First To Leave

Studies about gender-based differences in love relationships consistently show that men:

- ♥ Fall in love earlier in a relationship than women

and

- ♥ Take longer to get over the relationship after it breaks up.

I can think of six or seven men I know who were practically ruined by divorce. These men were so devastated that they let their businesses, finances, and health suffer seriously. I don't mean that they were ruined because their wives sued for heavy alimony settlements; I mean that these men were so heartbroken that they were no longer able to function normally.

One male friend of mine went from having a successful business and owning a beautiful home on a West Palm Beach golf course, to bankruptcy and foreclosure of the home within one year of his wife's departure. His world literally crumbled without her. The tragic irony is that the whole breakup was so avoidable.

His wife didn't just wake up one day and decide to leave him. It began when she felt neglected, almost abandoned, because he worked so many hours. She longed for companionship and romance, and she found it in the arms of an underemployed construction worker. Once she'd begun having an affair, she rationalized her guilt by convincing herself that she was in love with the construction worker. That's when she left her husband and home, and moved in with her lover.

She had no idea her husband loved her so much! Had she known, had he taken the time to *tell* her—instead of *showing* his love through his hard work—they might still be playing golf together under Florida's sunshine.

The couple's tragic scenario is all too common. Women search for evidence that their boyfriends or husbands love them, aching for written or spoken words of endearment. Every little "you're the greatest" or other compliment means so much to women. They replay these verbal hugs and kisses in their minds and relive the good feelings they evoke.

Women are auditory. They repeatedly replay answering machine messages that their men leave for them, analyzing and relishing the words and inflections in their voices. Pillow-talk and whispers of love are the equivalent of oral sex for women—sincere, loving words are the equivalent of a warm tongue caressing them into erotic arousal.

Women who aren't told "I love you" enough times, or who feel wounded because their men use harsh, critical, or sarcastic words, will feel unloved. They'll feel sorry for themselves, like little girls abandoned by their Daddies. They'll pull back and withdraw their own show of affection, thinking, "Well, if he isn't going to show love, then I'm certainly not, either!"

I think women, more than men, are afraid of rejection and abandonment. Men, of course, take many chances and risks by being the ones to ask for a dance or a date. Men may not like rejection, but they become used to it. The prospect of rejection doesn't scare them as much as it scares women.

Women also feel more insecure about being left alone. Although most women can take care of themselves financially, emotionally, and physically, there is a powerful fear in many of them about being left to fend for themselves. Perhaps it is biological, stemming from cave-woman days, when they absolutely depended upon men to provide food and protection for them and their children.

In response to this strong fear of abandonment and rejection, a woman pays super-sensitive attention to signs that a man is about to leave her or break off a relationship. If she senses his imminent departure, she heads off and dumps him first. Interestingly enough, men, more than women, show reluctance to leave relationships. Men usually leave only for extreme reasons, such as being fed up with a woman's alcoholism or mental illness. But a woman who feels unloved—because he doesn't say it enough and she's *convinced* that means he doesn't love her—will end the relationship before he has a chance to leave first.

After she's gone, he's shocked. Some men beg for another chance. Other men, out of pride or wounded self-image, don't ask for a reconciliation—even if they want one. Either way, the rejected man feels deep emotional pain. And the woman who left him is shocked to discover how wounded her former lover or husband is following the breakup.

Both partners may wake up, declare their love for each other, and reunite. Sometimes, the couple becomes even closer when they reconcile. Too often, however, a couple who has broken up once find their relationship forever fractured beyond repair. This cycle is the stuff that operas, movies, and romance novels are made of, but living through it is draining and damaging. It's easier and better to avoid it in the first place.

Love Stories and Mushy Movies

In romantic movies and novels, the heroine is pursued by a man who is hopelessly in love with her. Without her, he can't go on living, and he tells her so through tears, gifts, words, cards, and actions. *He must be with her.* She resists at first, but eventually capitulates to the strength of his ardor. In the end, they passionately kiss and ride off together into the sunset.

The books and novels don't take us beyond this moment, so we never get to see if the man continues his romantic pursuit once he's "got the girl." But in real life, the chase and the romantic words usually stop, or slow down, at this point.

Females are raised to believe that a man who really loves her is very vocal and persistent. Women not only enjoy being chased, they need it to feel loved. Being chased fits the mental image of true romance. "If he really loves me, he'll come after me," is the deep-seated belief of females raised on a steady diet of romantic movies.

A woman involved with a nonverbal male lover often feels insecure or unloved. She wonders why the man isn't showering her with compliments ("Am I not beautiful enough for him?") or words of adoration ("Doesn't he love me anymore?"). And when a women feel insecure and unloved, she may try to "test" her man's love simply in order to get a reaction.

Cheryl, for example, had been married to Bruce for almost a year. She missed the days of their courtship, when Bruce had told her every day how much he loved her. Now that they were married, she became obsessed with the need to hear more "I love you's" from her husband.

She would ask him, "Honey, do you love me?" and Bruce would reply, "Of course." And he meant it. As a man, Bruce assumed Cheryl knew he loved her. After all, he married her and spent all his free time with her. What more could she want?

Since Cheryl couldn't elicit her desired response from Bruce simply by asking him to say "I love you," she began to take action. She tried to make him jealous by mentioning business lunches she'd had with male associates, but Bruce only acted indifferently. Cheryl described how a female co-worker had asked her out for drinks, and Bruce had only said, "How come you didn't go out?" Now Cheryl began to wonder the same thing.

The next time her co-worker asked, Cheryl accompanied her to a local bar. The two women got smashed on margaritas and eagerly flirted with the men sitting near them. When Cheryl got home, it was nearly 11 o'clock and Bruce was sound asleep. The next morning, while Cheryl nursed her hangover, Bruce silently dressed and left for work.

This cycle continued for almost a month before Cheryl came in to see me. She was almost ready to have an extramarital affair, both to seek revenge against her non-expressive husband and because she craved romance. In therapy, she looked at how she'd pushed her husband away, and realized the extent to which she'd unknowingly contributed to the emotional distance she hated so much.

We brought her husband in for some couples counseling and found that he wanted love, reassurance, and affection as much as Cheryl did. Bruce was afraid he was losing his wife, and had retreated into an introverted shell to protect himself. Cheryl wanted Bruce to chase her; Bruce's self-esteem was wounded because he felt he wasn't making his wife happy. Once the couple understood each other's needs, the ice barrier between them melted.

Beware of the Come-On Man

Women who ache for expressive men often get trapped into a vicious cycle. I've seen it countless times, and I believe that the movie and music industries are largely responsible. Females who expect their men to be as emotionally expressive as Alan Alda, Phil Collins, Barry Manilow, or Tom Hanks invariably feel cheated, because most men don't communicate that way.

Don't get me wrong. There probably are some healthy, wonderful men out there who profess their sincere love enough to satisfy their women. But I've never met or even heard of such men. Every woman I've ever spoken with wants a little more romantic expression than she's currently receiving. And that makes women open targets for "come-on men."

We've all met him. Whether you're a man or a woman, you've met the "come-on man." I usually encounter him in grocery stores. He's the loudmouthed, ever-smiling guy who always has a compliment or a line ready for any woman in the vicinity. Some people might call him a "jerk." He's insincere, promiscuous, and very, very insecure about his masculinity. To prove himself, he tries to collect as many women's phone numbers, dates, sexual encounters, and girlfriends as possible.

The come-on man is exceptionally skilled at seducing women. Even the most wary woman is subject to his spell. Especially one who is dying to hear romantic expressions. He says all the right words and sends perfect red roses. She feels like the star of a romantic movie, with the come-on man playing the perfect male lead.

I know a very beautiful, intelligent, and accomplished woman who is constantly falling for come-on men. She knows what she wants from a man and is very adamant about it: She wants a man to chase her and to prove his love to her. Many men would love to be with Kristen, but most are too intimidated by her tall, statuesque beauty to approach her for a date. So Kristen goes out with the men who are most visible—the come-on men who constantly chase her.

Instead of pursuing a satisfying relationship with a genuinely caring man, Kristen wastes her time dating come-on men. She gets involved with them, often believing herself to be in love, and later discovers how superficial or promiscuous these come-on men really are. Until Kristen conditions herself to see how decent, genuine men also chase women—but in a quiet and sincere manner— Kristen will continue to be vulnerable to come-on men.

Body Insecurities: Am I Too Fat? Am I Too Flat?

It is normal for a woman to be critical about her physical appearance. It is perfectly ordinary for her to wish to augment, reduce, or otherwise change something about her looks—usually her weight, height, breast size, hip size, or hair color. As a psychotherapist, I've worked with many a beautiful woman who wailed that she had a "big nose" or "ugly teeth"—stupid, minor things that added to her unique beauty, but to her were major flaws.

One young woman in my practice, a stunning, aqua-eyed blonde named Terri, felt unlovable because she was "short and fat." At 5 foot 4, she was hardly short, and Terri easily fit into off-the-rack size 8 clothes. But she had been told by a previous boyfriend that her "butt was too big," a phrase Terri carried in her head constantly. She ignored men's approving stares, and told herself if she only could shrink the size of her bottom, she'd be worthy of a good love relationship.

Terri told me she was terrified of becoming involved with a man, because she didn't want him to see her naked. She was so afraid of being rejected and judged as "fat" that, when any new relationship began to approach the point where physical intimacy was imminent, she'd find an excuse to stop dating the man.

Terri and I worked through her body insecurities and her feelings of anger and grief surrounding the relationship with the boyfriend who had wounded her self-image. As part of her therapy, Terri began working with a personal trainer, and got to enjoy the feeling of firmer muscles throughout her body. The benefits were both physical and mental. With a newfound self-confidence, Terri was receptive to her next relationship, which eventually developed into a living-together arrangement with which she's very happy.

Terri's body insecurities were mixed with her fears about rejection and commitment. More commonly, a woman's body insecurities will interfere with her sexual enjoyment and physical pleasure.

One example was my client Kathy. At 42 years of age, Kathy could be described as "pleasant looking." She had a ready smile, expressive eyes, dressed stylishly, and wore her pretty blonde hair in a short, curly bob. Kathy was perhaps a little out of shape, but she was hardly "fat." Of course, in our society, a woman who wears anything over a size 5 often feels overweight.

Kathy did not enjoy making love with her husband. She described her sexual scenarios this way:

> I never make love during the day, when my husband can see me. And at night, if he wants sex, I make him turn out the lights before I take off my nightgown.
>
> Even in the dark, I feel so fat and ugly and I know he's wishing I were thin like those women in the girlie magazines. I lie there, feeling like a spotlight is shining on my cellulite, and wishing he'd hurry up so I could put my nightgown back on. He used to ask me to get on top during sex, but that position makes me feel even fatter! When I'm on top, I feel like my bottom and thighs are spread out really wide, and I can't move too well. I also hate the way my boobs sag when I'm on top. At least when I'm under him, my breasts look halfway decent!

There are many, many women like Kathy, who "freeze" during sex because they feel ashamed of their bodies. The negative self-talk accompanying poor body images ("I'm ugly," "I'm too fat," "My breasts are too small," etc.) makes sexual enjoyment impossible. True sexual pleasure occurs by focusing on the pleasurable feelings in your genitals and throughout your body. Arousal and orgasm happen in response to erotic, sensual thoughts. When a woman holds negative fantasies such as being too fat, and when she focuses on how much she dislikes her body, she is not paying attention to the pleasure of the moment. She is cheating herself, and ironically, she may later end up overeating in response to her sexual frustration.

Many of my clients, like Kathy, are *auto-sexual*, only having self-induced orgasms, using vibrators or their hands. There is nothing wrong with masturbation, of course. In fact, mutual masturbation adds to a couple's sexual pleasure. But when a woman in a committed relationship only experiences orgasm by herself, she is missing out on a whole world of stimulating pleasure.

Losing weight and toning up your body can enhance your love life. If you are unhappy with your weight or your body definition, I highly recommend a regular exercise program. You'll feel good about yourself for taking positive steps, and exercise will also increase your relaxation level. Both results will benefit you in the bedroom.

Just be sure to begin an exercise program to give *yourself* benefits. If you try to lose weight to please someone else, you're likely to resent that person and to end up abandoning your weight loss efforts. Remember that it is more dangerous to have up-and-down yo-yo weight patterns, than it is to be overweight. It is very hard on the heart and metabolism to lose weight and then to regain it. So, if you do decide to embark on a fitness program, check with your doctor first. And when you do start exercising and losing weight, plan on a lifetime of this new program.

A man can help his woman relax about her body insecurities, as well. He can ease her fears about being too fat or too flat by complimenting her on her beauty and saying, "I just love you breasts," or, "Your hips really turn me on." Of course, if he's insincere or sarcastic, these compliments will backfire and she'll feel worse. She may even verbally attack him if she feels really insecure.

But if a woman feels fat, don't hand her a diet or an exercise plan. She already has access to this information, and will feel even more unhappy if you imply that she's too heavy and needs to lose weight. Even if she says, "I'm too fat," never, ever agree with her. Don't fall into the deadly trap of saying anything about a woman's weight, unless it is a compliment. Your commenting on her weight is as devastating to her as her criticizing your penis would be to you. If you're really worried about her weight because of health problems, talk to her doctor. But never in any way imply that a woman is overweight or has any body imperfections. That is her biggest turnoff, because she'll feel you want another, more perfect woman. The more insecure she feels, the less she can relax and enjoy sex.

Instead, stroke her body lovingly and tell her how much you love her. Make her feel secure and loved, and she'll probably lose weight as a result. After all, if you provide love and romance, she won't need to turn to food for comfort anymore.

Body Insecurities About Her Genitals

Women also feel insecure about vaginal odors, and so are often uncomfortable when men want to perform cunnilingus—oral sex—on them. If, as a man, you notice your wife or your girlfriend is having difficulty achieving orgasm when you "go down" on her, a number of problems probably exist. First, women have been bombarded with advertising and other sources of information that their vaginas have distasteful, fishy odors. They worry that their men will be turned off if they discover how badly their vaginas smell or taste.

Many men find the vagina's natural odors to be very arousing—and if you do, be sure to tell this to your partner. Repeatedly. If there is an especially strong, unpleasant odor from her vagina, she's probably got a health problem and you shouldn't be down there with your mouth in the first place. Just as with her weight, she's aware if there's a problem with her vagina, so you don't necessarily need to say anything about an unusually strong odor. If you are worried, however, phrase your concern *very delicately*. Remember how sensitive she is regarding this issue.

When a woman's clitoris is stimulated on a steady basis, she'll usually achieve orgasm very quickly. If she doesn't, it might mean she's very uptight or worried, and is not concentrating on the pleasurable feelings. She might be focusing on you, worried that your tongue, hand, or arm is getting tired. It's a good—no, a great—idea to periodically say something like, "I get so turned on by doing this to you," or, "I just want you to relax and enjoy this" during oral sex. Say something so she won't feel guilty about all the work you're doing, and she'll actually orgasm faster and better.

If you've reassured her about her body insecurities, and she's still having trouble achieving an orgasm, there are two other possible reasons. If she's had too much alcohol or other mood-altering drugs, she may be numb to orgasm. This is the female equivalent of a man's difficulty getting an erection after too much drinking.

In the absence of too much alcohol, however, it may be the technique the man is using that is the problem. In later chapters, we'll go over ways to satisfy a woman sexually. Meanwhile, be assured that it is normal not to know exactly how to please a woman this way. Females have been socialized never to discuss their sexual natures. Many women don't even know what sexually pleases them, since their whole focus has been on pleasing men, and not themselves. And, of course, every person is different in their sexual tastes and desires. Each couple has to learn how to please themselves and each other.

Vaginal Exercises

Many women are worried about being "tight enough" to please their men. Females worry that their vaginas may be too loose, too lubricated, or too dry. In Chapter Twelve, you'll read about sexual positions that can help ease this concern. Men, of course, have analogous fears about genital inadequacy. In fact, a new medical specialty is enlarging penises with fat transplants and prosthetic implants.

Women don't need surgical intervention to make physical changes in their genitals—they just need a vaginal exercise program. *Kegal exercises* strengthen the muscles behind the vaginal walls. The benefits of regular kegal workouts are enormous:

1. Because of increased muscle strength, the orgasm contractions are more powerful. Most women report more pleasurable orgasms following regular kegal exercises.

2. The increased vaginal muscle mass gives both the man and the woman increased pleasure during intercourse, because the penis feels bigger and the vagina feels tighter.

3. The woman's confidence in her sexual "prowess" increases with her kegal fitness program. Just as someone who has a fit body from exercise feels confident, so does a woman who is a regular kegal exerciser.

4. Kegal exercises are insurance against incontinence later in life. Women who keep their vaginal muscles strong through regular kegal workouts are less likely to experience urinary leaking when they become elderly.

5. Women who regularly practice kegal exercises have easier vaginal child deliveries. Most obstetricians and Lamaze instructors recommend that pregnant women engage in kegal exercises, because the strengthened vaginal muscles help push the child during birth.

Kegal exercises are accomplished this way: The next time you urinate, contract your vaginal muscles until the urine flow stops completely. Then relax the muscles and allow the urine flow to return. Then, stop it again. You've now located the muscle group involved with kegals. Next, try contracting and relaxing the muscles while not urinating.

Contract and relax this muscle group several times a day, doing sets of 10 in the beginning and working up to sets of 25 or more. The beauty of this exercise is that you can accomplish it while driving or while at work. If only the rest of our bodies could be exercised so easily and discretely!

The bottom line in the whole discussion regarding female body insecurities is that a woman's fears about whether her body is "good enough" interfere with her pleasure and relaxation in the bedroom. A man can help by regularly reassuring her about how good she looks and how great she feels. A few well-timed words go a long way in helping her feel sexually confident. And when she feels good about herself, she'll stick with her man and go out of her way to please him.

The Fairy Tale Princess

Those of us who were raised on fairy tales can identify with the princess in most stories. She's the one who was adored for her beauty and sweetness, who later married Prince Charming, and lived happily ever after.

Just as men see themselves as "The Knight," who wants appreciation and admiration, women's romantic mythological identification is with "The Princess." Deep down, each woman wants to be adored and pampered as though she were a fairy tale princess. The persona of a princess is that of a special, beautiful, and very feminine girl. Even women who seem tough and masculine hold deep desires to be viewed as this ideal type of female.

Men who understand these desires are adored by women. If a man takes the time to pamper a woman with little "princess presents," such as tender words, surprise kisses gently placed on the neck, or staring in her eyes and saying, "You are the most beautiful woman in the world," she'll be deeply grateful.

Some men worry that if they compliment their women too much their heads will swell with vanity, and they will leave them for other men. All people feel insecure from time to time, and no one wants to be rejected or abandoned. But a man who is afraid that he'll lose his wife or his girlfriend if he boosts her confidence will end up losing her if he doesn't. She'll either leave him emotionally by avoiding spending time with him, or she'll leave him physically through a divorce or breakup.

I had a boyfriend who was afraid to compliment me. I overheard some friends telling Paul, "Gee, Doreen looks really great tonight." Immediately, Paul told them to be quiet, hissing at them, "Don't ever tell her she looks good. She'll get a big head over it."

Paul, like many men, had never been one to give many compliments. But he had always told me how much he loved me, and that had sufficed. About nine months into our relationship, however, he stopped even saying, "I love you." I didn't understand! I would tell him that I loved him, and he wouldn't reply with the same words. I asked him, "Do you love me?" and he'd nod, but he wouldn't say the words.

What was going on? He refused to tell me. Like most women, I need to be told that I am loved. Paul was being cruel, I felt, by withholding what I most wanted. I didn't ask for much from this man, but this was a non-negotiable issue, as far as I was concerned. I told him how troubled I was by his lack of verbal expression, and how he was in danger of losing me because of it. He still wouldn't say the words.

I broke up with Paul. I moved away from him, back to my friends and family in California. It was extremely difficult, but I couldn't be with a man who refused to provide for this basic need. And, wouldn't you know it, after I moved away, he called me and told me how much he loved me. He said that he had been afraid to tell me, something about the grief he had still been enduring over the breakup of his marriage two years before. He was afraid that if he became really vulnerable and expressed how much he'd fallen in love with me, how much he needed me, I'd somehow manipulate or take advantage of him. But, by withholding expression, Paul lost me and our once-beautiful relationship.

The saddest part of all is that I now know that Paul—like most men in such situations—was silently screaming his love. I just wasn't listening. He was showing, not saying, "I love you." I didn't know, at that time, how much men express love non-verbally. After Paul called me and confessed how much he loved me and how deeply he was hurt by my leaving him, I began researching men's expressions of love.

Expressing feelings is a risk, especially for men, who have received so much training about being strong and invulnerable. Just as a woman may feel foolish or fake when she attempts to "show," instead of tell, a man that she loves him, a man will feel like he's speaking a foreign language when he expresses his love. The world of verbal expression is her turf, one in which she feels naturally comfortable. He, on the other hand, can feel like an impostor when he's discussing love and romance. No one likes to feel unsure of themselves. Especially men. And unsure is how they feel when they attempt to discuss their feelings.

It's a balancing act: We need to express feelings to each other, both verbally and nonverbally. I, and most women, need to be with a man who tells me he loves me. I won't insist that a man continually compliment me, because I know that's unnatural and unreasonable. An occasional compliment, yes. But I figure even Cindy Crawford isn't complimented nonstop by her husband, Richard Gere. And she's a world-class beauty! So, as long as my man says "I love you" regularly and makes me feel appreciated with his nonverbal actions, I'm content.

In my relationship with Michael, my "significant other," I feel satisfied because he goes out of his way to make me feel loved and wanted. Michael tells me he loves me several times a day, and he constantly demonstrates his love with countless little and big things. He hugs me from behind and nuzzles the back of my neck while I'm cooking, and he swoops me into his arms and gives me a big, wet smooch as we pass each other in the living room.

Michael stares in my eyes and says, "I love you—a lot," with utmost sincerity. He holds doors open for me, and pays for dinner at restaurants. Michael gives me cards with sweet inscriptions such as, "I look forward to a lifetime of love together." And he holds me tightly every night before we fall asleep.

I communicate my appreciation for his expressiveness, so Michael knows how much I love his tender words and thoughtful actions. This is important: If your man acts in a way that you like, you must give him positive reinforcement. Unless he knows you like something, he probably won't repeat it too often.

Tell him, "I love it when you [fill in the blank]. . ." and he'll be happy to repeat the behavior often. If you try to manipulate him to be expressive, it won't work. Which one would you rather hear: "You never do anything romantic!" or, "Sweetheart, I love it when you're romantic"? Which statement would inspire *you* to behave romantically?

Chapter Four

Love is Child's Play

"Romance must be different every time. If she does my favorite thing every time, it would lose its romantic quality. It would not put me in the mood. Romance must be full of surprises!" —43-year-old married man

Remember when you fell deeply in love? When the emotions of new love hit you so strongly that you thought about your beloved nonstop? When you felt as though you were in a romantic movie, or floating slightly above earth level?

During the initial stages of courtship, several factors create these sensations. First, there's the novelty of meeting someone new. Everything you learn about that person is a revelation, with no monotony or repetition to bore you. Newness is exciting and takes your mind off mundane details at home or problems at work.

Second, there's the "blank slate" factor of a new lover. The new partner hasn't revealed anything negative . . . yet. During new relationships, we also tend to ignore any red flags of negativity; the new lover seems wonderful—almost perfect. We project all our fantasies about the ideal man or the ideal woman onto our new partner. We fantasize that this new person will be the cure to our ills and the savior to our wants.

Third, when we begin dating a new person, the entire relationship is an ambiguous mystery. "Will this turn into a serious relationship?" we wonder. Insecurities may surface: "What if he (or she) doesn't want a relationship with me?" These questions and fears actually contribute the high of a new relationship, because our senses are tuned into a "heightened stress response." Like an animal fixated on a prey, our focus is almost entirely devoted to the new lover.

When I think of new love relationships, I imagine a couple walking hand in hand through a county fair or on a beach. The couple in my mind is focused on each other—the rest of the world has ceased to exist for them. They're smiling, laughing, maybe even skipping a bit. In other words, there's a childlike sweetness to their behavior.

New love is filled with childhood innocence and sweetness. Yes, there's a sexual undercurrent with new love, but it's mixed with excitement and a sense of adventure. It's also combined with fun and play.

We all were children at one time, and we all knew how to play. Growing up, we attained positive qualities associated with adulthood: a sense of responsibility, work, ethics, and compassion. But we still retain the positive attributes associated with childhood: a sense of adventure, delight at surprises, emotional sensitivity and the enjoyment of playing or having fun.

Most of the time—especially at work—we stay in an "adult" frame of mind. It is neither safe nor appropriate to express our childlike side when we're trying to make a living. Our childlike qualities are reserved for leisure time. People who can express the child and the adult parts of themselves regularly suffer from less stress than those who always stay in the "responsibility" mode.

We all need to play. For years I've given workshops and lectures on stress management, at corporations both large and small, throughout the country. The message I most try to impress upon stressed corporate employees is the need to balance work with leisure time. If people give themselves "time off" to play on the weekends or after work, they'll feel more energetic, creative, and effective when they return.

Many people complain that they lack time for fun or leisure. After work, they're busy with home and family responsibilities. On weekends, they catch up on chores and errands. They view fun as a luxury and an optional activity. And they wonder why they feel tense, stressed, and burned out.

Fun is not an optional activity to be wedged into two-week increments during the annual vacation. It is a necessity for refueling our spirits and our energy. The child within us needs to come out and play regularly, at least once a week. Remember the old adage, "All work and no play makes Jack a dull boy"? My version of this phrase is, "All work and no play makes Jack a frustrated, unhappy boy."

Remember how you felt when your Mom or Dad were happy? You felt good. And isn't it nice to see your spouse in a good mood, maybe whistling or singing? It feels good to be with people in happy spirits. Other people enjoy it when you're in a great mood as well. Having fun, relaxing, and enjoying yourself are ways to stay "up" and happy. Because your mood has such a large influence on those around you, you're actually doing others a favor when you enjoy yourself. Remember that the next time you feel guilty about relaxing or having fun.

The fun-loving child within you comes out when it's safe and when you're relaxed. That is why you enjoy being around people you've known for a while. You've learned you can relax, be silly or spontaneous, and just be yourself around them. Your "child" knows it's okay to come out around these friends.

In a relationship where there is much tension or hostility, the child rarely comes out in either partner. The child is afraid of being ridiculed or punished, so he or she hides and cowers in the corner. When this occurs, the couple loses their ability to play, have fun, and be spontaneous.

Spontaneity is vital to a love relationship. Without it, the couple walks on egg shells to avoid arguments. The partners are uptight and worried about saying or doing the wrong thing. There is no relaxation, and there is especially no fun.

I've Grown Accustomed To Your Face

It's easy to look at a couple, observe their behavior and body language, and get a very accurate picture of the state of their relationship. Look at the couple sitting across from you at the restaurant or driving next to you on the road. Are they looking at each other? Are they engaged in active conversation? Are they smiling or laughing? Do they seem to enjoy being together?

Newly-in-love couples always seem to be having fun. They're high on the relationship and on the feelings of new love. As the partners spend more time together, they ease into a routine. They have to! If they stay "high" from being in love, they won't get any work done; they'd be emotionally drained and exhausted.

"Habituation" is the term that describes becoming used to, or accustomed to, a situation. In habituation experiments, a subject's brain waves are monitored while a loud bell is rung. The first time the bell clangs, the subject's brain waves register a startled reaction. The second, third, and fourth times the bell is rung, the brain waves still show activity. But eventually after the bell continues to ring repeatedly, the subjects adjust to the noise and their brain waves don't show any more excess activity. This adjustment is "habituation."

(Interestingly, when schizophrenic subjects go through the same experiment, they never habituate to the bell's noise. Every time the bell is rung, they respond as though for the first time. Their brain wave activities register identical heightened reactions from the first to the last ringing. Other studies support the conclusion that schizophrenic people don't habituate to repeated stimuli.)

Whether it means growing accustomed to the smell of the bakery in which you work, or getting used to the noise of your car, it is normal for mentally healthy people to habituate. When you come home from work, for example, you don't really look closely at your furnishings. You know that your couch and table are there, but you've habituated to their presence, so you don't pay much attention to them. Now if a change occurs, such as the furniture has been rearranged or a bright new pillow placed on the couch, you'll notice. This is because habituation allows you to compare your memory of the situation to the current situation. If everything's the same, you won't react. If there is a noticeable change, you will observe it.

The same is true in relationships. We habituate to the other person's presence, appearance, and behavior patterns. Habituation has gotten a bad rap in the popular media, however. Remember Lucy Ricardo or Alice Kramden complaining that their husbands were "taking them for granted"? The television sitcom wives wanted to be continually wined and dined by their hubbies. They felt bored—probably because they had no real purpose or direction in their lives—and blamed their husbands for their discontent.

But think about the couch example. Just because you don't hug your couch every time you come home doesn't mean you don't appreciate it. It doesn't mean you're thinking of running off with a new, younger couch, does it? You enjoy your couch's benefits every time you sit or stretch on it, don't you? Just like you and your partner appreciate each other after all this time.

What Kind of Fun Personality Do You Have?

We all enjoy novelty and excitement, because it makes us feel alive. The *types* of excitement we seek depend a lot on our personalities. In other words, different people seek different levels and types of fun. I have a friend who loves to hang-glide and sailplane, and does so weekly. I went sailplaning with him once, and thought I was going to die from fright. On the other hand, I find going on national television or giving a speech to be pleasant experiences—and these are things that he dreads!

Some people take physical risks, and others take emotional risks. Approaching a stranger and starting a conversation is an emotional risk. You risk being rejected or humiliated, because you don't know who this person is, or how he or she will respond. But you also risk making a new friend or business acquaintance. Bungee-jumping is a physical risk, fraught with the possibility of breaking your neck, but also of achieving an incredible adrenaline rush.

Are You a Physical or an Emotional Risk Taker?

There are different types of physical and emotional risk takers, as well. I think many differences are gender specific, probably because of our different physiological makeups. Maybe you've noticed—I certainly have—that at amusement parks, men congregate toward the types of rides where passengers "fall," whereas women prefer rides that spin in circles.

Within relationships, women and men take different emotional risks. Usually, the man initiates the relationship. He asks for the first date. He initiates sex. He usually is the first to say, "I love you." And he traditionally is the one to suggest marriage. Along the way, the man is risking rejection—a big emotional risk.

What emotional risks do you take in your relationship? How comfortable are you taking emotional or physical risks?

There are theories that people who have a high need for stimulation take more risks in life. The theory is this: Some people's brain chemistries are set like a car engine that idles at a fast speed. These people need extra stimulation and excitement simply in order to achieve normal levels of arousal. Where some people would find a bicycle ride exciting, these people need to go hang-gliding to feel any form of arousal. It's as though they need to put "extra salt" on the food of life, because their excitement "taste buds" are a little numbed.

Everyone's tastes in food, fun, and excitement are different. If your partner's favorite activities don't appeal to you, you have a few choices. You can learn to enjoy them. You can just go along and "grin and bear it." You can stay home and create your own brand of excitement. Or you can discuss and create compromises.

The most important point is to create an awareness of each other's tastes in fun. Fun, within couples, doesn't mean spending every day at Disneyland or going river rafting. It means enjoying time together.

When we were first married, my ex-husband and I took a trip to the Hawaiian islands. There I learned about our different tastes in fun. My ideal vacation was basking in the island sunshine. My husband, however, thought going to museums and tourist spots was the height of vacation fun. Obviously, we couldn't do both simultaneously . . . or could we?

Our choices were to:

♥ alternate the two activities, spending part of the day outdoors, and part of the day in museums

or

♥ spend our days apart and individually pursue our pastimes

or

♥ attempt to combine the two activities.

What we ended up doing was to compromise. We rented a convertible Mustang and drove from museum to museum with the top down. When we got to a museum, I decided whether to accompany him or to take my towel over to the beach next to the museum. It worked out well, and we both had fun together. Too bad we couldn't compromise as diplomatically in other aspects of our marriage.

Where Has All the Fun Gone?

Fun can constitute a planned activity, or it can simply be spontaneous enjoyment of each other's company. Either way, fun is vital to the physical and emotional health of an individual and a relationship. Without fun, we shrivel into gray, depressed shells of our true selves.

Many people postpone fun, thinking, "I don't have time for frivolous activities right now."

Consider these couples who have let the fun go out of their lives:

The Outer-Focused Couple

Cathy and Brian had been married for five years, and both held middle-managerial positions at large corporations. Their work lives were intense—filled with pressures and lots of overtime. The couple supported each other emotionally, with Cathy listening sympathetically to Brian's complaints about his department head, and Brian offering Cathy advice on how to handle employee difficulties. When it came to their careers, they had much in common.

However, Cathy and Brian's devotion to their jobs left little time for recreation—unless it had to do with work. Brian learned to golf because executives were "expected" to recruit new clients out on the golf course, and Cathy entertained her corporate clients with lavish meals at restaurants. But these activities were work, not play. Brian couldn't relax and be spontaneous while golfing; he had to watch what he said to avoid offending clients. He even let important clients "win" golf games. Cathy, too, felt frazzled after most client lunches and dinners.

The couple's work life had consumed their sex life. Exhausted at night, and in a hurry in the morning, Brian and Cathy had little time or energy for sex. Although they loved each other very much, their passions were focused on getting promoted at work. Couples like Brian and Cathy, who have their attention pulled by work or family concerns, often "postpone" romance, passion, and sex. They put it off until their schedules are clear—which, of course, they never are.

Brian and Cathy have two ingredients working in their favor: First, they have a common interest in their respective careers, which functions as a shared passion and fuels a precious friendship between them. Second, at five years, their marriage is still relatively new. However, in five or six years, either Brian or Cathy is going to be less driven at work and will crave more fulfillment at home. In other words, their habit of postponing passion won't work much longer.

The Sibling Rivalry Couple

Stan and Rhonda had been married for 15 years. "Fifteen lo . . . n . . . g . . . g . . g . . . years," Stan described with a grimace.

Rhonda rolled her eyes and responded, "Not half as long as it's been for me!"

The couple engaged in one put-down after another, each trying to outdo the other in a strange form of game. Rhonda believed that if she put Stan down enough, she'd look good to others. Stan, too, thought he'd somehow appear strong and victorious if he publicly insulted his wife. The couple didn't realize that others saw them as a unit, as a couple, and not as two individuals competing to see who was correct or right. Others plainly saw Rhonda and Stan as an unpleasant couple and tried to avoid them.

On closer examination, it was obvious that Rhonda and Stan held a deep affection for each other. They were both simply feeling insecure about their individual worths. Their mutual put-down routine was a habit constructed out of this insecurity. They were competing with each other in the same way that young brothers and sisters compete for their parents' attention.

The Bored Couple

Marcia and Henry, like many couples, had married because they were in love. When Henry met Marcia, during his senior year and her junior year in high school, he told his best friend that it was "love at first sight." Soon after meeting, they were a steady couple—and have now been together for 26 years.

Their oldest child is married and lives 750 miles away. Their youngest lives and attends college in another state. Marcia and Henry are alone every evening, and they don't know what to do with all that time together.

When Henry comes home from work, Marcia spends her time preparing dinner. He reads the paper; she cooks. They eat dinner in silence while watching television. She does the dishes and he takes a nap on the couch. Later, they watch television until bedtime. Then they go to bed and sleep. All evening, they've exchanged 10 or 12 words consisting of, "Please pass the butter," or, "Would you rather watch the news or the movie of the week?"

Henry and Marcia are not unhappy, but both feel lethargic and bored. Their lives revolve around work, chores, and television. The only time they really talk is when one of the children telephones or visits. Sex is predictable and routine, with no variation on technique, place, or time.

The Anxious Couple

Ed and Patty were both worried. The economy in their town had soured and many people were out of work. Patty hadn't been employed during their 22-year marriage, so she really didn't have any marketable skills. And Ed's employer had just announced the impending layoff of 60 employees.

It seemed there was always something to spoil the couple's otherwise-good life. Before this problem concerning their financial future, Patty's health had been a large source of concern. And before that, one of the kids had gotten into trouble with the law. There were problems stretching back throughout the couple's entire marital history. When would they finally have the peace and happiness for which they'd worked so hard?

All of the couple's concerns and worries were legitimate and worthy of their attention, of course. But in working with Ed and Patty, I found that they amplified their problems to the point where the anxiety and worry were needlessly overwhelming. They focused on problems instead of trying to look for creative solutions. They lost sleep and frequently suffered from insomnia over their concerns. Ed and Patty had literally worried themselves sick.

Because of this constant tension and anxiety, the couple had devoted no time to leisure or to having fun. They hadn't vacationed in 15 years. They rarely left the house except to go to work, church, or shopping. And they never laughed or joked.

The therapy I suggested for this couple consisted of stress management and relaxation techniques, such as those outlined in Chapter Nine. They learned of the necessity of fun and relaxation, and how it could help them solve their problems. The couple also took the time to set financial goals and to create a budget—two steps that made them feel more in control of their lives.

The Depressed Couple

During the early part of Bill and Karen's marriage, there were some real financial struggles. Bill was a full-time law school student and Karen worked as a medical secretary to pay the rent for their small apartment and to keep food on the table. Although both were busy, they spent many evenings snuggling on the couch, watching television, and eating Chinese takeout.

Then Karen became pregnant. Both Karen and Bill were thrilled at the prospect of having a child, but each worried privately about the impact this change would have upon their lives. The pregnancy changed everything sooner than they expected.

When Karen was diagnosed with toxemia during her second trimester, her doctor insisted that she stay home and rest until the baby's birth. Bill dropped out of law school "temporarily" and took a job as an insurance adjuster to make ends meet. He never did go back to school, and he and Karen eventually had three more children.

As a senior adjuster, Bill makes a moderately high salary, has good benefits for the family, and can look forward to a stable retirement pension. But he never recovered from his lost dream of being a high-powered attorney, and most of all, he never lost his strong desire to be self-employed. "I work for a huge company," Bill explains, "and I've just never felt comfortable having so many bosses, rules, and regulations. I always dreamed of having my own law practice, where no one could tell me what hours to work or when to take vacations."

As Bill nears his fortieth birthday, he knows he'll probably work at his insurance company until retirement, a fact that makes him depressed. "Don't get me wrong, I love Karen and the kids, " he explains. "It's just that I thought my life would be a lot different. I really saw myself making much more money, having a big house, and mainly having a lot more freedom and personal time. You know, the country club and golfing lifestyle."

When a man has employment difficulties, money insecurities, and career problems, it deeply affects his sense of maleness. "A real man is in control of his career and his money," is the unconscious logic of most men. When a man feels out of control of his career, it makes him feel less masculine—as though he's failed.

This sense of failure leads to big problems in relationships, especially in the bedroom. In fact, most of the male clients I've seen over the years have entered therapy around their fortieth birthdays—one of the most vulnerable times for men. Mid-life crises happen when we realize that we're approaching middle age, and that we have not met all our goals and objectives. We take stock in our lives, at around age 40, and ask ourselves, "Am I happy with my life?"

Bill and Karen entered therapy because, as Bill became more depressed, the couple felt their union disappearing. "He won't tell me what's wrong!" Karen complained to me. "He always shared his problems with me, but lately he's been so distant. And he hardly ever wants to make love anymore." She began to cry. "I guess he thinks I'm too old. I guess I don't turn him on like I used to!"

I explained the dynamics of male mid-life crises to Karen, telling her that his distance had nothing to do with his feelings toward her. I knew, from my private sessions with Bill, that he had a deep commitment to his marriage. The problem was that he was questioning his masculinity—because he saw himself "stuck" in a (to him) mediocre career.

Karen had been knocking herself out trying to arouse Bill sexually. She'd tried lingerie, losing 15 pounds, and putting blonde highlights in her hair. Nothing seemed to work. When I advised Karen to be patient and to give Bill time to privately console himself, she agreed to give it a try.

The Color-Me-Gone Couple

Sheila and Frank had been married for 12 years, but they'd probably only spent half that time together. Frank's job as a sales manager sent him traveling on a weekly basis. He'd be home for weekends, and then back at the airport each Monday morning.

"When I get home Friday evenings, I'm really glad to see Sheila," said Frank. "But I'm exhausted from traveling so much during the week, so I usually head straight to the bedroom to take a nap when I get home. I know Sheila would prefer me to take her out to dinner and to catch up on the week's activities, but I just don't have the strength."

Sheila looked down at her clenched fists. "By the time Frank recovers from his week's activity, it's Sunday afternoon. I really only get to be with my 'real husband,' the Frank I know and love, from Sunday afternoon until Monday morning." She looked at him sadly and said, "I really wish you'd get a different job."

"We've been through this a thousand times, Sheila. Times are tough, and there's no way I'll find another job that pays what this one does."

"I don't care. I just want my husband at home."

It was apparent that the couple had been at a stand-off for some time. Both felt misunderstood and unappreciated, and these feelings were creating more barriers in their marriage.

Any time a couple spends time apart—whether it's an hour or a month—the individuals develop a *separateness* from the experiences and the activities taking place. When the couple reunites, there's a warm-up period that occurs before the normal closeness and emotional intimacy is reignited. Couples like Frank and Sheila, who spend a great deal of time apart, are constantly in a state of warming up. They are getting to know each other again, and are spending little time in the phase of feeling close and intimate. In a way, this feeling of reunion can seem special and romantic. But overall, a couple needs to spend enough time together so that they're not constantly in the warm-up phase.

The Bitter Stand-Off Couple

When Mark and Dolores married 15 years ago, it seemed that nothing could interfere with the couple's deep love for each other. Devout Christians and active churchgoers, Mark and Dolores felt their unfaltering faith would immunize them against the harsh world.

But now the couple's marriage seems more like a wake than a celebration. Mark and Dolores rarely speak to each other. Lovemaking is relegated to rushed, silent sessions once or twice a month.

What happened? At one time, the couple had made love on a daily basis!

Ten years after they'd married, Mark was struggling at work. His company was merging with another, and his middle-management position was in danger of elimination by the new company. Mark's solution was to prove his worthiness by working twice as hard. His stress level soared as he clocked 65-hour weeks.

One evening, he and his secretary, Stephanie, had put in a 12-hour day. To show his appreciation for her hard work, Mark took Stephanie out to dinner. The relaxation of the wine and pasta that followed such a stressful workday made Mark feel giddy. Mark was horrified by the attraction he suddenly felt for Stephanie. After all, he was a married man and a devoted father. Still . . .

Two weeks later, Mark and Stephanie ended up in a hotel. He was devastated and decided that the only way to regain his honor was to admit everything to his wife. Mark and Dolores decided that God wanted her to forgive Mark for his mistake. They prayed that their marriage would be healed.

Mark's job was salvaged with the merger, and he resumed working normal hours. Dolores, however, was still struggling with her husband's admitted affair. She couldn't relax during sex any longer. She cried during the day and her moods alternated between fury and despair. Every time she'd bring up her feelings to Mark, he would tell her to pray. But Dolores felt betrayed, and she showed Mark her hurt and anger by refusing sexual relations with him. Mark, in turn, felt rejected.

Five years later, the couple's stand-off has crystallized into a habitual way of dealing with each other. The built-up resentment and anger have put Mark and Dolores at a crossroads: They need intensive marriage counseling, or a divorce will be inevitable. Neither is happy.

The Passion Makeover

Some couples, like Mark and Dolores, have allowed resentment and anger to build up to dangerous levels. These painful emotions often show up first in the bedroom. It is difficult to be turned on by someone who has hurt your feelings. Often, counseling is necessary to peel away years of resentment. But you can also take steps to refuel your original passion, and the first step is in rediscovering how to have fun with your mate.

Putting fun back into a relationship takes time, patience, and a willingness to experiment to discover what works and what doesn't work. In other words, there is some effort involved in rediscovering fun. But the effort is worth it, because fun is a central component of passion and a satisfying love life. Fun is the shot in the arm that will revitalize your relationship and create heightened erotic pleasure.

Did you ever see a makeover in a magazine? The kind where they show a photo of someone without makeup, with an ugly outfit and stringy, dirty hair? The "before" and "after" shots are always dramatically different, and it's sometimes hard to believe it really is the same person!

A relationship without fun, and without passion, is like the "before" shot. You're going to give your relationship a "passion makeover" by adding fun into your daily life. The most important type of fun—like the base foundation of makeup in a cosmetic makeover—is the simple, unplanned kind. The embellishments and the finishing touches in your makeover are the more planned types of fun, like outings, activities, and vacations.

Let's start with the foundation. Often, I've found people "forget" how to have fun. They really do! After years of having their noses to the grindstone, many people lose sight of how to enjoy themselves. They also succumb to routines, and repeat the leisure activity over and over until it loses the luster of novelty.

Below are some suggested ways to have fun with your spouse or your lover. Some of these activities should be "mentally noted" and acted upon spontaneously when the time is right. Other activities take a little forethought and preparation. As you give yourself a passion makeover, keep in mind that having fun is a "positive habit" that each person and each couple needs to learn. At first, add a small dose of fun on a daily basis—10 minutes to a half hour of fun per day is a good starting point. Then work up to an hour or more of fun every day. Don't save fun for the weekend or your once-a-year vacation. A passion makeover means applying fun to your life on a daily basis!

Fun and Passion, Here We Come!

Can one partner infuse fun into a relationship, or does it take both partners to have a passion makeover? The answer is, *you* can start the "fun ball rolling" and inspire your partner to play and to have fun with you. Of course, timing must be considered. You don't want, for example, to try to start a fun time when she's getting ready for work, or when he's cooking an exotic meal. Look for opportunities on weekends and evenings to try one of these fun ideas:

- ♥ Tickling each other. Don't be surprised if this leads to some hot lovemaking!

- ♥ Pretending you are teenage lovers that have been left alone in the house

- ♥ Having a fun, friendly pillow fight

- ♥ Going on a picnic in a secluded location

- ♥ Going to a comedy club

- ♥ Feeding each other chocolate treats

- ♥ Chasing each other around the house

- ♥ Playing hide-and-go-seek

- ♥ Going bicycling together

- ♥ Going for a long walk together

- ♥ Checking into a local hotel, either for a leisurely week-end complete with room service, or for a "quickie"

- ♥ Going to a drive-in movie

- ♥ Having Sunday champagne brunch in bed

- ♥ Playing on the park playground equipment

- ♥ Joining a sports team together

- ♥ Surprising each other with a trip out of town.

Most of these fun ideas are rooted in childhood-type play. Remember that the little girl or the little boy you once were is still alive and kicking inside you. That little child has a sense of fun, daring and adventure. She or he will take your adult hand and teach you how to add more fun to your life.

Make laughter, play and fun one of your goals and regular activities. Think of it as emotional calisthenics that keep your relationship in top shape. Laughter eases tension and helps us to relax. We'll learn in the chapters that follow how important relaxation is to a truly satisfying relationship—both in and out of the bedroom.

Chapter Five

Romance Is Priceless, But Not Expensive

"To me, romance is having a man do something for you totally by surprise and because he wants to make you happy. Something like leaving you notes or messages when you're not home. Anything spontaneous that is not in a day-to-day routine." —*35-year-old married female*

Romantic gestures are symbols. Whether the symbol is a handwritten love note or an expensive piece of jewelry, the result is the same. Everyone appreciates a thoughtful gift or a loving word.

Let me share with you one of the most romantic gestures I have ever known. It is the story of how a friend of mine asked his wife to marry him.

At the age of 28, Bob was diagnosed with cancer. His girlfriend, Heidi, stood by him and accompanied him to his doctor visits. She lent a great deal of support, for which Bob was extremely grateful. When his cancer went into remission and Bob's doctor declared him "in the clear," Bob knew the first thing he wanted to do to celebrate his new lease on life: He wanted to marry Heidi.

Bob decided to surprise Heidi with a romantic weekend away. He picked her up for lunch on a Thursday afternoon. He had arranged with Heidi's employer to allow her to take two days leave from work, and had also enlisted the help of Heidi's roommate, who had packed a bag of Heidi's favorite clothes and toiletries. The bag was in the trunk of Bob's car when he fetched her at the office. Of course, Heidi didn't know anything of Bob's plans.

"I have to stop at the airport for a minute," Bob said as he pulled into the airport's short-term parking lot. Heidi, who was accustomed to Bob's running work errands during their lunch hour, didn't think anything of it. That is, until he opened the car trunk and pulled out their suitcases. "Surprise, sweetheart," he said as he kissed her.

An hour later, they were on the way to New York City. A stretch limousine met them at John F. Kennedy Airport, and took them to their suite at the Plaza Hotel. Heidi was thrilled, but there was even more in store for her. At dinner that evening, he'd arranged to ask the woman of his dreams to marry him.

Their quiet corner of the restaurant was perfectly romantic. A violinist played a sweet solo for the couple, and Bob petted Heidi's hand gently. When the violinist stopped, the waiters were right on cue. One waiter put a champagne flute in front of Heidi, while the other swept a beautiful, candlelit, pink-icing cake on the table.

"Will You Marry Me?" was inscribed in bold, magenta frosting on the cake, and as Heidi blinked unbelievingly at the question, she noticed a shiny glimmer in the champagne glass. A beautiful diamond ring!

After Heidi recovered enough to say, "Yes! Yes!" the violinist returned and played for the couple, who were now kissing passionately. Bob and Heidi then returned to their room and consummated their engagement with sweet, romantic lovemaking.

I love that story. To me, the romance stems from the amount of effort Bob put into surprising Heidi. Yes, the flight, Plaza suite and limousine were all elegant, expensive touches. But the most moving part of the whole scene was the obvious love, thought, and care behind it.

I know Heidi would have been equally pleased to go to any restaurant and have the "Will You Marry Me?" cake and engagement-ring champagne flute placed in front of her. That was the most clever part of Bob's production.

The best romantic present of all is a symbol that says, "I care."

The Gift of Love

When do you give a gift to your lover? Birthdays and holidays are obvious answers. One of the best ways to surprise your partner and to inspire romance is to give him or her a token gift or to perform a thoughtful act "for no special reason." In talking with men and women about romance, I heard many comments underscoring this desire to be surprised on "ordinary days."

One man told me he loved it when his girlfriend surprised him by preparing a bubble bath when he came home from work after a particularly difficult day. He felt completely spoiled by her royal treatment: a warm bath, wine for both of them, soft music and candlelights illuminating the bathroom. His girlfriend even scrubbed his back, which led to a long, luxurious lovemaking session.

Another woman told me how much it meant to her when her husband would leave little love notes under her pillow. I also spoke with a woman who was thrilled to come home from work one Friday evening and find that her husband had arranged for the children to spend the night at Grandma's house. He'd prepared dinner and had even rented a romantic movie they'd both wanted to watch.

A man I know who is extremely handsome and successful, and could probably date any woman he wished, told me why he is so crazy about his current girlfriend. "She goes out of her way to make me feel special," he said. "It's not any one thing she does in particular. It's about a thousand little things, like giving me backrubs, buying my favorite ice cream, and watching Monday night football with me. She's turned into my best friend, and that inspires me to show her that I love her, too."

When we think of "gifts," we usually envision pretty wrapping paper, bows, and boxes. But, let's face it, discretionary income is becoming more difficult to find. Besides, expensive gifts aren't necessarily the best gifts. Think, for a moment, about what presents you've enjoyed the most over the years. What made you happy about them? How much they cost, or the thoughts behind them?

The truly valuable gifts that stay in our memories are valuable because of their meanings. In interviewing thousands of men and women for this book, the one thing that impressed me the most was that *everyone* wants a satisfying, monogamous love relationship. They just want that relationship to be with the "right person."

That right person is usually defined as someone who is compatible, easy to get along with, stimulating, thoughtful, loving, and fun. By giving the "gift" of thoughtful surprises, you become the "right person," the fantasy lover your partner desires. You become loving, compatible, and fun.

You can't demand that someone love you, and you can't force someone to be romantic. But since a desire for romance and love is a basic part of human nature, you can tap into your partner's romantic energy and *inspire* the other person to behave romantically.

We all prefer the company of people who make us feel good about ourselves. We enjoy being around positive, uplifting people. So, one gift to give your lover is the gift of being a pleasant person with whom to spend his or her life. You can genuinely keep yourself in an up mood by taking care of getting your own needs met. This means doing things that make you happy.

When you're satisfied and feeling good—because you're taking care of yourself—people will naturally be attracted to your warmth and genuine happiness. You'll shine from within, and it will be a pleasure to be near you. You won't be demanding or complaining, because you'll be satisfied. You'll be irresistible!

Romantic Symbols and Gestures

Very few of the women interviewed for this book mentioned mere flowers as a romantic symbol. And no one, male or female, told me that presents put them in a romantic mood.

Many people told me that they liked to be surprised, and that they enjoyed it when their partners put effort and initiative into planning a romantic interlude. The *what* of the romantic evening wasn't that important; it was the *how* that mattered. The romantic setting could be at a restaurant, a five-star hotel, a drive-in theater—or at home. What matters is that someone cared enough to think up an original plan.

Here are some romantic moments that remained in the memories of men and women with whom I spoke:

♥ He picked me up for our date, held open the car door for me, and there was a single red rose sitting on the passenger seat for me.

♥ She arrived to pick me up at the airport, wearing   nothing but a long coat and a G-string bikini.

♥ He made dinner reservations at the restaurant where we'd had our first date.

♥ She surprised me with two great tickets to the ball game. Then, when we went to the game, she was as much into the game as I was.

♥ I had to go out of town for a business trip. Not only did he take me to the airport, but he packed a really romantic card into my suitcase.

♥ He introduced me to his friends as, "The love of my life."

♥ She asked me what my favorite meal was, and then the very next night, she prepared it for me.

♥ She had this great-smelling oil that she rubbed all over my body. She gave me an all-over body massage that left me feeling relaxed all evening and into the next day.

♥ I mentioned that I wanted to see the new ballet company at the performing arts center. I wasn't hinting or anything; I just mentioned it. Imagine my surprise when he produced two tickets for us to the ballet!

♥ He made a tape of all my favorite songs.

♥ He knew I was on a diet, so I thought it was really sweet that he brought home nonfat frozen yogurt.

Some of these romantic gestures cost money, but most are inexpensive or free. The common thread in all these "gifts," of course, is they that they convey expressions of love. The gift givers took the time to figure out what would make the other person happy. Then they orchestrated the romantic gesture into a surprise.

When you surprise someone with a romantic gesture, you'll inspire them to return the expression. You're not surprising them in order to manipulate them into behaving romantically—believe me, they'll sense the manipulation and will respond to that instead of to the romantic gesture. You're surprising them out of your genuine desire to express tender feelings.

The Gift of Appreciation

Deep inside all of us, there is a longing to be appreciated. We want our specialness to be loved and noticed. We want to be respected and accepted. When we are with a love partner who believes in us, it inspires us and gives us courage to take risks that can ultimately lead to success.

The old adage: "Behind every great man is a great woman" is very true. And I also believe that behind every great woman there is a great man. In the tremendously stressful world of careers and business, having emotional support at home provides us fuel and a secure foundation. It really *is* a jungle out there, and having a loving partner at home creates a sanctuary that lends an escape from the world's craziness.

Home is like a pit stop from the Indianapolis 500 we race every day. At home, we get our emotional, mental, physical, and spiritual tires rotated and our oil checked and changed. If we don't get revived in the pit stop of home, we'll never survive the race. And a great relationship is like high-octane fuel. It boosts our energy and our creativity.

We've all experienced being distracted at work because of an argument with a lover or a spouse. What's most upsetting about these types of quarrels is that we feel misunderstood and "wronged." We feel unappreciated—and it hurts. Making up occurs when we explain our positions to each other and apologize.

Deep down, everyone knows he or she has special qualities and characteristics. We like people who acknowledge these "hidden talents." Your lover will think you are very clever for recognizing his or her "specialness."

Think about your partner for a moment. What is it about him or her that is special? Why have you chosen to be with this person, over every other potential lover in the world? Even if your partner is not your ideal mate or dream lover, something is keeping you with this person. Why? What are those special qualities?

Once you've written down a list of your partner's attractive characteristics, it's time to express your appreciation. You will reinforce and encourage your partner to display these positive qualities every time you tell him or her what you like. This is not manipulation. You are simply rewarding your lover for his or her attractive characteristics, and in this way, making your lover feel good. When your lover, in turn, appreciates your appreciation, a positive cycle follows.

There are many ways to express these feelings. Of course, showing your approval through loving actions is the best way to let your partner know how you feel. But it is also important to spell it out.

You can write your partner a letter, saying exactly how you feel (keep it positive and don't get sidetracked) in honest and sincere language. Your letter is a way to let your lover know that you approve of and admire those special qualities. My father wrote my mother such a letter last year, and I know it meant a great deal to her.

Short notes and cards work, as well. Jot down a phrase such as:

♥ You are such a thoughtful person

♥ You are so beautiful

♥ Your creativity is incredible

♥ You are the world's smartest woman

♥ Thank you for helping me solve the problem. I couldn't have done it without you.

Surprise your lover with this little note of appreciation by putting it in a surprising place: the bathroom drawer, under the pillow, on the car dashboard, in a lunchbox, in a suit pocket, in the medicine cabinet—some have even put it in the morning newspaper! Use your imagination and have fun with it.

If writing isn't your style, you can tape-record your thoughts onto a cassette, with appropriate background music. Put the tape in your partner's car tapedeck for a real surprise.

You can write your lover a poem or a song. Artistic-types can create a painting, sculpture, photo-essay, or mosaic that captures your feelings and says, "You're very special to me. I love you."

Bragging about your lover to other people, when your lover is listening, is another way to express your admiration and appreciation. Even if it embarrasses your partner a bit, your outspoken approval will be endearing. Tell others how proud you are of your partner's accomplishments and special qualities. Talk about the positive qualities of your relationship.

As mentioned before, romantic gestures are most appreciated when they are least expected. Most people count on receiving gifts from their partners on birthdays or during the holidays. But getting tokens or gestures of appreciation on "ordinary days" makes loud statements of love and approval. And they're incredibly romantic.

Giving of Yourself

An important romantic gesture is sharing your time and attention with the one you love. Time is a shrinking resource for many of us. Our attention is pulled in several directions at once, as we attempt to accomplish several things simultaneously.

In new relationships, we focus much attention on our new lover. We look at the person closely and listen attentively to every word. We laugh at the new lover's jokes and feel empathy when he or she expresses pain. Over time, when the novelty wears off and we reenter reality, our attention is given less to our lover and more to day-to-day concerns.

When you make yourself pay attention to your lover's words, you are giving the priceless gift of your time and attention. Look your partner in the eye when listening, and try not to interrupt. Nod or say, "Mhm," to show that you are listening. Smile or laugh at your partner's jokes. Make supportive physical contact, such as holding hands, rubbing your partner's neck, or caressing his or her back.

Do all this and see what happens. Your partner will begin to open up and share more feelings, thoughts, and experiences with you. Pretty soon, the two of you will be engaging in some interesting, exciting conversations. You will feel closer, and by engaging in meaningful conversation, much of the romance of the relationship will begin reigniting.

Talking with your partner on a deep level is the heart of romance, and Chapter Six delves into this topic in more detail. By sharing your hopes, dreams, frustrations, and aspirations with your partner, you recapture much of the magic of a first date. Hope, after all, is what sparks a union in the first place. Hope that this is Ms. or Mr. Right. Hope that you've found the love of your life. Hope that you two can pursue your dreams hand in hand. Talking with your partner about hopes helps recapture that fresh energy that initially united you.

I've listened to many couples who are caught in a time-deficiency trap. Working parents are especially strapped for time and energy. Their attention is diverted to careers and to kids, leaving little room to devote to each other. The husband and wife are exhausted. They spend little time discussing things other than money or children, and after a while they lose touch with each other.

Other couples are trapped in a superficial giving cycle. Let me explain: The husband works and works to buy and buy nice things for his wife. She appreciates the gifts, great house, vacations and other things her husband's salary earns. But what she really wants is romance, and time alone with her husband. So she complains. He resents her complaining, thinking she doesn't appreciate how hard he works. She feels abandoned; he feels unappreciated.

Clearing the calendar to spend undistracted time with each other is vital. You and your partner are ever-evolving people, with hopes and thoughts that grow and change with time. By taking time to "check in" with each other, you keep up with how your lover is doing. You may rediscover what an interesting person your lover really is. Instead of seeing your wife merely as the woman with whom you live, or as the mother of your children, you'll remember what a vital, exciting person she is. Instead of viewing your husband as a hardworking provider, you'll recognize him as the enthusiastic, sensitive man with whom you originally fell in love.

Couples who live with children, roommates, or parents need to arrange regular time alone. If money is tight, make arrangements with friends who have children. Exchange baby-sitting services for one weekend a month, and then plan on devoting time and attention to your partner that weekend you are alone together.

The object of giving gifts is to make the other person happy. Therefore, anything you do that makes the other person happy is, by definition, a gift. Women can give men the gift of nonverbal communication, of silently expressing approval and admiration. Men can give women the gift of verbal outpourings of love and affection.

When you make your partner happy, that in itself is a reward. Also, your partner will express gratitude for your "gift" by seeking to please you in return. The gift exchanges may not always be an even one-for-one; but if you take the first step, and give the first "gift," eventually your partner will follow suit. Remember that deep inside him or her is the person with whom you fell in love.

Here are some "love gifts" to give to your partner. Give generously, without expectations of reciprocation. Of course, don't demand appreciation for your presents. Instead, be gracious in your gift giving and remember that a true lady or gentleman gives freely without expectations. If your partner has any awareness or manners at all, he or she will show appreciation. It may not be immediate, but your partner will express gratitude with like favors.

Love Gifts To Give Your Partner Tonight

♥ A foot rub

♥ A back massage

♥ Allowing your partner to control television viewing

♥ Perfuming the bed sheets

♥ Listening to your partner attentively

♥ Resisting the urge to complain, to correct your partner, or to be negative in any way

♥ Making sure you are well groomed and attractively dressed

♥ Offering to pour and to serve after-dinner drinks

♥ Turning the bed covers down for your partner

♥ Taking the time to learn a funny joke, and sharing it with your partner

♥ Asking your partner questions about how his or her day went

♥ Performing oral sex on your partner

♥ Preparing and serving a special dessert

♥ Kissing your partner sweetly on the hand or cheek

♥ Surprising your partner with a love note hidden under a pillow or in a bathroom drawer

♥ Whispering "I love you" into your partner's ear

♥ Turning the telephone off, and the answering machine on, for the evening.

Chapter Six

Whisper In My Ear...

"I want my husband to say nice things to me and to say how beautiful I am and how he realizes my good points. But I also want him to tell me he loves me for other reasons than my looks. Also, I like it when he doesn't push me for sex and can just be satisfied with talking with me."
—33-year-old married woman

While surveying men and women for this book, the most significant trend to emerge was how the sexes differ in *communicating* love and romance. The majority of women surveyed said that they love to hear words of love or compliments about their beauty or their intelligence. *None* of the men mentioned words as a turn-on.

To men, romance is communicated through actions and sights. A woman shows a man she loves him by taking the time to dress attractively. He also loves it when she smiles at him and gazes in his eyes.

How can men and women communicate romance, when they're speaking two different languages? Only through understanding and creative compromise.

Being aware of the gender-based differences in communication styles is a significant first step.

The Look of Love

If you're a woman, you can set the mood for romance by trying to look your best, whether you're relaxed in front of the television set or out on the town for dinner and a movie. You're giving your man a gift equivalent to a dozen red roses when you take care of your appearance. You can be in jeans and a sweater and still look great, just by checking your makeup and hair, and by choosing a flattering outfit.

Throw away your ugly flannel nightgown and replace it with a feminine nightie. Your man will appreciate it if you dress in lingerie and other sexy outfits, as well. Believe me, you don't need a perfect body to arouse a man with lingerie. They love skimpy, lacy outfits, and their eyes will focus on your best features.

Wear makeup at home and keep your hair looking clean and brushed. Check your teeth regularly, and wear contact lenses instead of glasses around the house. Don't make a big deal about your beauty regimen by discussing it with him, and certainly don't start an argument if he doesn't seem to notice your improvements. He *does* notice. He's just not auditory, so it doesn't occur to him to remark on your looks. Talking about his thoughts and feelings is as foreign to him as dressing well on your leisure time is to you.

By taking the time to look attractive, you are speaking volumes of love to your man.

Then, after you look great, be sure to look at your man. He needs your eye contact while he's talking, just as much as you need him to tell you that he loves you. Give him your full attention, as you did on your first date. Smile at him and laugh at his jokes. You're not being passive or manipulative by engaging in this nonverbal communication. You're simply speaking his language!

Pillow Talk

A man who wants to keep the woman in his life happy must learn to verbalize romantic words. Now, here's the tricky part: Since it's not natural for a man to express emotion—after all, his whole life he's been socialized against doing so—how does he verbalize what he feels and still sound sincere?

Many times, men will compliment women and be accused of using a "line." Their words will sound rehearsed or insincere. Does this mean the man is saying the words in order to seduce a woman into bed, or to manipulate her emotions? Or is he simply awkward and afraid, and unable to articulate well?

There are clues that a woman can use, including trusting her instincts, when deciding whether a man is a womanizing cad or not. Most can intuitively decide whether a phrase is sincerely meant. The sincere man's voice is slow and full of pauses, and his voice may even crack. He swallows hard and his breathing becomes fast and shallow.

A man shouldn't be intimidated by this unspoken communication. If he sincerely means the compliment or the love phrase he's saying, the woman will know it. And she'll be extremely appreciative—and will hopefully show her appreciation in his visual language!

It is difficult to do any job without the proper tools. In communicating romance through visual means, a woman will have to go out and buy lingerie and new makeup. The equivalent task for a man would be to add new words and phrases to his vocabulary.

Here's a list of "emotional" words to use when communicating with your woman. Use only those words that describe how you're feeling. Please don't hide or disguise your emotions. She's impressed with honesty (using diplomacy, tact, and thoughtfulness, of course) more than anything else. Men are sometimes reluctant to discuss feelings that may make them appear vulnerable. They're concerned that the woman will perceive them as signs of weakness. The truth is, women love to be trusted and needed. You'll touch her deeply by opening up and sharing your problems, concerns, hopes, and dreams with her.

"I Feel"

♥ Happy, pleased, elated, excited

♥ Confused, bewildered, perplexed

♥ Shy, bashful

♥ Angry, furious, enraged, upset, annoyed, agitated, betrayed, perturbed, irritated

♥ Worried, troubled, concerned, anxious, insecure, frightened, afraid

♥ Turned on, aroused, excited

♥ Bored, restless

♥ Tense, stressed

♥ Relaxed, carefree, optimistic

♥ Embarrassed, ashamed, remorseful, guilty

♥ Confident, secure, trusting.

What is the point of discussing feelings? It is not to elicit solutions or help from your wife or your girlfriend. Women, make a *big* note of this: Men do not want your help in solving problems. They simply want you to listen. To men, it is considered a sign of weakness not to be able to solve problems on their own. Now, of course, if a woman discusses her problems with a man, the man will offer her advice and suggestions. But, the reality is that neither men nor women want help. They simply want empathy and a friendly, non-judgmental ear.

When a man discusses his feelings openly and honestly with his woman, their relationship improves dramatically. A woman is naturally very intuitive, probably because of the act of childbearing, which demands that she instinctually be aware of her baby's needs. When you are troubled, she knows it immediately. She may think you are upset or displeased with *her*. If you share your feelings and thoughts with her, it eases her mind. She now knows the source of your mood, and she knows that it isn't her!

To please a woman completely, you'll say romantic phrases—again, with heartfelt sincerity. Here are the kinds of things she's aching to hear. Choose the phrase closest to your real thoughts and feelings, and then edit the sentence as needed. Put your arms around her, lift up her hair, kiss her neck, and whisper one of the following potent phrases in her ear:

Romantic Phrases She Wants To Hear You Say

♥ I love you

♥ You are the most beautiful woman in the world

♥ You are the perfect woman for me

♥ I want us to grow old together

♥ I can't imagine being with any other woman than you

♥ You are my dream come true

♥ You are the love of my life

♥ When I look at you, my heart beats faster

♥ I love you so much I feel my heart will burst

♥ I'm so glad you love me

♥ I don't know what I'd do without you

♥ Will you marry me?

♥ Will you marry me all over again?

♥ I'm so glad you married me

♥ You look beautiful

♥ You look like you've lost weight

♥ You have the most beautiful (breasts, legs, face, etc.) I've ever seen

♥ You smell great

♥ I love the way you look.

Try one or two of these phrases tonight and see what happens. She'll show her appreciation for your job well done by giving you a kiss, a hug, or a smile. Just always be sure to be sincere. And do not overuse the phrases, or they'll lose their impact.

Women also love "pet names"—terms like "darling," "sweetheart," and "love of my life." Be careful with the pet names "doll," "doll face," or "sweetie," however, because some women find them corny or sexist, and may be turned off.

Other Ways To Communicate Romance

When you want to tell the other person how you feel, or when you want to surprise your love partner, a greeting card is often the best choice. There are cards conveying most sentiments and thoughts these days. If you don't find a card that exactly conveys your message, get out your pen and cross out a word or a line and insert your own. The card will have more charm that way. Best of all would be to buy a blank card and write a personal message.

Surprise your lover with cards. Lots of them. They are one of the best, and least expensive, tools for romance that exist. Leave the card in unexpected places around the house, or mail it to your lover—even if you live together!

Cards give men and women the best of both worlds: The messages satisfy her auditory need for words, and the card itself captures his desire for love to be shown through actions. And since both sexes appreciate surprises and spontaneity, giving cards is satisfying and fun.

Notes, like cards, are spontaneous expressions of appreciation and love. When my boyfriend began putting little one-sentence notes under my car's windshield wipers, I really enjoyed it. Sometimes, he'd put a cartoon that he knew I'd like and just draw a heart with his name next to it. Other times, he'd write a simple phrase like, "I love you. Have a great day." It got to the point where I'd look at my windshield wipers first, when I went to my car. I anticipated each note as eagerly as I would a Christmas present.

Try putting romantic notes in your lover's briefcase or suit pocket, or on the refrigerator. Write "I love you" in lipstick on the bathroom mirror. Or draw the words in the sand when you walk on the beach or in the park.

Little "I love you" or "I'm thinking about you" telephone calls are also romantic. Leave a quick phrase on your lover's answering machine, and it will stand out among the other messages as an uplifting boost. A one-minute "I just wanted to tell you how much I love you" telephone call will mean a lot to your lover. If he or she has a *private* voice mail, E-mail, digital pager, or fax machine, you can leave a high-tech romantic message.

Sending a single red rose to your partner's place of employment also speaks volumes, but this may backfire. Some people don't appreciate having their personal lives spill into their business lives. I learned this the hard way. When I sent my then-husband a rose at work for Valentine's Day, he was a little embarrassed. I think the reverse-sex roles had something to do with it (his male co-workers had teased him a bit). But he told me that he enjoyed it.

Communicating During Sex

Silent sex. Loud sex. Everyone has different tastes and styles about talking or making noises during intercourse. Styles can also change from time to time; for example, sex may become louder after the couple has had a few drinks.

Communication during intercourse can be verbal and nonverbal, and can set the tone for highly romantic—or highly erotic—sex. If you want romantic lovemaking, kiss continuously during intercourse. Hold hands and have your entire bodies, down to your toes, locked together. The man should be deep inside the woman, with slow strokes that keep his penis deep at all times.

For more erotic nonverbal communication, the sexual strokes should be faster, with more intense thrusting. The man can suck the woman's nipples and bite her neck. The woman can run her hands over the man's body and fondle his scrotum.

When a man moans during sex, his woman's need to hear reactions is fulfilled. To a woman, a man's moans are like applause that compliment her performance. A man, too, is aroused when the woman is obviously turned on during lovemaking. Both partners should moan when they feel pleasure. Each sound conveys the message: "I like what you're doing—don't stop."

There is also evidence that emitting deep, throaty sounds and moans increases one's pleasure during intercourse. There is a school of thought in psychology (which has been applied to actors studying the Stanislavsky method of acting) that making the primal sounds of moaning has cathartic and relaxing effects.

Some of my most erotically-charged memories are of when my boyfriend conveyed intense, overwhelming pleasure as he was having an orgasm. As a woman, I'm extremely auditory and can recall sounds, voices, and music in my "mind's ear" with incredible precision. When I remember my boyfriend's moans, it's a very arousing thought. And I know many other women who feel the same way.

Should words be spoken during intercourse? Later, we will examine talking about fantasies during lovemaking. But for now, let's just acknowledge that every person has different tastes concerning conversations during sex. In general, I believe an occasional, "Oh, that feels so good" moan or murmer enhances the couple's pleasure. But a steady stream of narration can break each partner's ability to concentrate on their individual feelings and pleasures. This is especially true for women, who are unlikely to climax solely from intercourse, and who need to focus on their bodies instead of being distracted by their partners' voices.

Most women are turned off by slang words and foul language, in and out of the bedroom. Men who enjoy rough street talk during intercourse need to discuss this topic with their lovers, at a time when sex is not imminent. If you're a woman who doesn't appreciate hearing about "fucking" or graphic descriptions of genitals, and your man uses these words regularly, it's best to inform him of these feelings. Many men are offended by street language, as well. But if you both find "talking dirty" to be arousing, then certainly sprinkle the words liberally into your sexual repertoire!

Finally, in my survey of men and women, both sexes said that they found music to be very romantic and stimulating. Try playing music (not the radio, because the commercials will interrupt your mood and concentration) during lovemaking. You'll find the music may inspire new rhythms. Whether you choose classical symphonies, romantic ballads, or energetic rock, the background music will enhance your lovemaking considerably.

Communication Crossovers

We've seen how men are primarily visual, and women auditory. There are, of course, exceptions and crossovers to this general principle. Men also like to *hear* compliments and words of praise, and women want to be *shown* love, too.

Both sexes enjoy compliments. And, yes it's true, men and women both need to be shown love, as well as told about it. Men, for example, like phrases that convey admiration, respect, trust, loyalty, and appreciation. The "Knight" inside every man wants confirmation that he's successfully accomplished his mission, whether that means keeping his princess happy or winning her undying devotion and admiration. He works hard to earn the reward of his woman's appreciation.

Here are some phrases you may use—again, only if you sincerely mean them—that convey the feelings that your man longs to hear:

- ♥ You are so clever

- ♥ What would I do without you?

- ♥ I'm with the smartest man in the world

- ♥ I know you'll find a solution to the problem. You always do

- ♥ I will always be by your side

- ♥ No matter what, I will stay with you

- ♥ I never want to be with any man other than you

- ♥ I really appreciate all the hard work you do

- ♥ I admire your ability to solve problems

- ♥ Your muscles are so strong

- ♥ I love the way you make love to me

- ♥ You satisfy me every time

- ♥ I trust you completely

- ♥ You're my hero

- ♥ You're my king.

These phrases mean as much to a man as the statement, "You are the most beautiful woman in the room" means to a woman. If they feel awkward to say, that's okay. Just as long as the sincerity rings true, your man will appreciate the words as much as he would an expensive gift. Remember that men typically don't receive the emotional and social support that women friends provide for one another. A man usually receives his sole support from his wife or his girlfriend, and he relies on you to provide steady doses. If you regularly boost his spirits and his ego, he'll be very fulfilled and won't even dream of leaving you for another woman. It's that important to him.

Also, women should be aware of how much men "read" the expressions women wear on their faces. If you are a woman, try to stay aware of your facial expressions when you're around your man. While looking at him, it's important to smile when you feel pleased, because your smile speaks louder to him than your words. When you're walking around the house, try to break the habit of wearing a frowning expression, because he may misinterpret this to mean that you're upset or angry. If nothing else, remind yourself that frowning uses more facial muscles than smiling typically does. And as we age, the frowns become part of our permanent wrinkles and lines.

Similarly, women have a need to receive some nonverbal conveyances about love and romance. Men can show their amorous feelings through actions that speak loud and clear. Besides the traditional ways that men show affection, here are some ways that their women will "hear" their feelings without their saying a word:

1. When you're out in public together, don't stare at or flirt with other women. This includes not being overly friendly with waitresses, hostesses, and cashiers! If you see a beautiful woman while in the company of your wife or your girlfriend, take a quick mental snapshot of the other woman and look at her in your mind's eye. Don't say a word to your companion, even if she says something like, "Isn't that a beautiful woman over there?" It's a trap you don't want to fall into! Say instead, "What woman?" and you'll win your lover's affection for the day.

2. Hold your wife or your girlfriend's hand as often as possible, whether at the dining table, in the car or watching television. Michael always holds my hand, and it makes me feel close to him, even if we're not exchanging words or glances.

3. Help her around the house with chores, such as dishes or laundry. Michael dries and puts away the dishes that I wash every night. Even though this may not sound romantic, to me it's a gallant gesture that I really appreciate.

4. Help her with her car. This can include surprising her by washing her car or the windshield, or filling the tank with gas. Advise her when you notice that the tires need air, or better yet, take the car and fill the tires for her!

5. Give her your undivided attention when she's talking. Be patient and don't finish sentences for her, or interrupt her. Convey to her that you think her ideas and goals are important. When she tells you about a problem, listen emphatically. Don't offer solutions unless she specifically asks for them; women don't want advice, they want empathy. Just listen. Laugh at her jokes. Show her how important she is to you, and that you love her for her mind. If you do this, she'll love you in return!

Better Left Unsaid

We've devoted a lot of time to discussing the phrases men and women want to hear. But there are also many phrases that should be avoided. Basically, anything that conveys the opposite of respect, admiration, and approval to a man, and any words communicating the opposite of adoration or cherishing to a woman, should be avoided.

Phrases and Topics Never To Discuss

1. Avoid discussing past relationships. Nobody wants to visualize their lover making love to someone else. And it's too easy to sound as though you're comparing your present lover to your past one.

2. Never say anything negative or derogatory about your lover's body. Even if you believe your lover will be grateful for your suggestions and advice, resist the urge to say anything that is not complimentary. A women should never, ever joke about a man's penis. If she says, or even implies, that his penis is small, the man's ego will be irreparably damaged.

A man should never say, or imply, that his woman's bottom is too big or that her thighs are too flabby—even if they are! All women are painfully aware of their body fat. If you tell her she's fat, she'll *feel* fat. If she feels fat, she won't feel sexy or in the mood, and you'll both miss the opportunity for great sex. Similarly, never tell her that her breasts are less than perfect, even though every woman feels that she's too small, saggy, big, or droopy.

3. Don't say anything negative about your lover's family, even if he or she says something negative about yours.

4. Don't bring up negative topics or arguments in the bedroom. This room should be sacred and off-limits to ill feelings.

5. Don't go on and on about how beautiful, handsome, clever, etc. the person you see on television seems to be. If you go overboard with admiring words for this stranger, your lover may feel slighted.

6. Similarly, avoid saying anything positive about your lover's enemies or arch-rivals. For example, if your wife has always been jealous of her sister, avoid saying things like, "Gee, your sister looked great today, didn't she?" Your wife will hear that you really mean, "Gee, I really would like to sleep with your sister."

7. Women should avoid this phrase like the plague: "I want to help you get in touch with your feelings." Men do not want you to help them with anything, especially getting "in touch" with their emotions. Remember, they've had it pounded into their heads since childhood that "real men don't cry." He'll open up to you when he feels a non-judgmental, no-pressure opportunity.

8. Men will do well to avoid any phrase smacking of an order. Phrases beginning with, "I want you to . . ." are better replaced with, "Would you please . . ."

9. Both sexes will be rewarded for using "Please" and "Thank you" and other examples of polite manners when talking with a lover or a spouse. Even though you've been married for 20 years, your spouse still deserves your respect. In fact, he or she deserves it much more than strangers or casual acquaintances do.

10. Don't joke about, argue with, correct, or put down your lover in the presence of others. Nobody enjoys criticism, but you can at least accept it and listen to it privately with your lover. But in public, a bad joke or an insult directed toward your lover will make her feel "not cherished," and will make him feel "not respected." Any possible laughter you'll gain from your audience for such a joke will be at the expense of your lover's good feelings.

11. Finally, in the heat of anger, be very careful of the words you choose. Insults and below-the-belt jabs are easy to hurtle when you're upset, but the damage is long lasting. Remember, women can replay "audio tapes" in their heads and rehear hurtful phrases with the accuracy of a Memorex tape. And men who hear words of disrespect can nurse long-lasting resentments. It's very important not to use someone's confessed secrets against them during an argument. If this happens, your partner may never again confide in you. And that will block the precious emotional intimacy you previously shared.

You'll recall that in my survey, *both* men and women revealed that romance is extremely important to them.

Communication, both verbal and nonverbal, is a cornerstone of romance. Words and actions can destroy a relationship, but they can also heal the wounds of lovers who have grown apart.

Part II

Recapturing Love's First Blush

Chapter Seven

Falling In Love All Over Again

> "I love it when my husband sets the atmosphere for a romantic evening at home together. He'll dim the lights or light candles for dinner. But most important, he'll make me feel special, and then I forget about everything else. Our best times are when he just focuses on me and ignores his pager or the telephone."   —45-year-old married woman

Sarah and Bradley sat in my office on a rainy afternoon, looking as miserable as the weather. Both had their arms tightly crossed, as though they were defending themselves against a deadly enemy. They rocked in their separate reclining chairs nervously, looking at anything but each other. Sarah and Bradley had "lost that loving feeling," and they weren't sure that they could ever regain it.

"Do you remember the first time you saw Sarah?" I asked Bradley.

He replied that he did.

"What first attracted you to her?"

Bradley's answer was easy. He said that it was Sarah's eyes, which were a beautiful blue-green color, and which had looked so lovingly at him. And the fact that she paid attention to every word he said.

"When did you know you'd fallen in love with her?"

"The first time I met her, I knew." Bradley said the words slowly. "I knew she'd be my wife and that we'd always be together. She was the sweetest, gentlest woman I'd ever met. She was absolutely beautiful." He turned his chair to face Sarah momentarily. Then he looked down with a mournful expression.

Sarah looked equally grim.

"Sarah, what first attracted you to Bradley?" I asked.

"His smile," she replied with a frown, not realizing the irony. "Bradley *used* to make me laugh. I loved the sense of humor he used to have."

"Do you remember when you knew, without a doubt, that you loved Bradley?"

Sarah's face softened and her voice grew small and childlike. "It was the night he told me he loved me. We were making love—oh, it was so good!—and he held my head in his hands and said, 'I love you so much.' My heart just melted and I knew I loved him, too."

She looked at Bradley and smiled sweetly. He stared in her eyes and mouthed, "I love you." He then rose from his chair and walked over to Sarah, who was now crying. He bent over her and embraced her. Sarah wrapped her arms around her husband and held him tightly.

The couple *remembered* the early feelings of love in their relationship. This is one of the first important steps in *recapturing* those feelings, as well.

Do you remember what first attracted you to your mate? Do you recall when you fell in love with your partner? The qualities that first sparked romance are still there. They're covered with a dusty buildup of anger, resentment, and disappointment, but they're still there.

The unfortunate cycle that occurs in relationships is that both partners withhold love, affection, humor, and other positive emotions as a self-protective measure against hurt. Every time you feel disappointed in your new love, you put up a little barrier so that the next disappointment won't hurt as much. You begin to distrust this person just a little bit. "Maybe this isn't my one true love," a little voice of doubt begins to whisper.

Holding back positive emotions such as love, spontaneity, and affection, is a normal reaction when we feel emotionally in danger. When we perceive the other person as not having our best interests at heart, how can we trust that person?

The trouble is, after the first person begins withholding expressions of love, the other partner follows suit. Charleen and Larry, for example, were trapped in the web of a cold war. It began early in their relationship, when Larry insisted that his ex-in-laws be invited to their wedding. Charleen didn't understand why Larry wanted an ongoing relationship with his ex-wife's family, and she protested. She also secretly wondered if she should really marry this man.

After the wedding, Charleen cringed as Larry's ex-in-laws hugged him and kissed him on the cheek. How bizarre, she remembered thinking. I would never associate with my ex-husband's parents, and I especially wouldn't invite them to the most important day of our lives! Charleen felt sorry for herself, feeling that Larry didn't respect her feelings.

She drank quite a bit of champagne at the reception, and to spite Larry, danced with the best man most of the evening. Larry glowered at her from across the room, and then, in retaliation, danced with Charleen's younger sister.

The couple's wedding day set the pace for the remainder of their marriage. Each felt justified for being standoffish. Charleen felt Larry should make the first move toward warmth and intimacy. Larry just assumed he'd married a bitch, and didn't even try to regain the closeness he'd felt toward Charleen during their dating period.

The Peace Accord— Step One

Whenever we feel a painful emotion such as hurt or betrayal, our "inner child" appears. We all were children once, and during that time we formed many of the philosophies we carry with us as adults. The way we related to our brothers and sisters influences how we interact with love partners. For example, girls who competed with brothers are likely to compete with male lovers. Boys who felt responsible for sisters may have difficulty trusting the self-sufficiency of their wives.

I've seen many relationships destroyed because hurt feelings and fears of abandonment were masked over with anger or emotional distance. The partners are afraid to reveal their true feelings—afraid that honesty will make them vulnerable to a second attack. Instead of leveling with her husband, the hurt wife calls her best friend for consolation. Instead of coming clean with his wife, the injured husband spends the evening at a sports bar.

Marriage counseling largely consists of guiding couples to be honest with each other. The therapist urges partners to discuss and to "work through" old hurts. This removes bitterness and resentment. Then the couple is counseled about ways to maintain an honest atmosphere. As misunderstandings arise, the couple is advised to clear the air immediately.

The couple involved in marriage counseling learns constructive ways to discuss disagreements. Accusations and insults are replaced with direct and assertive statements about "what I believe" and "how I feel." The partners listen carefully to each other, and then cooperate and negotiate to create solutions fair to both partners.

Marriage counseling is for couples in all stages of matrimony. Dating, engaged, newlywed, stand-off, and divorcing couples can all benefit from checking in with a licensed marriage counselor or with a psychologist. Marriage counseling is the equivalent of having your car tuned up, or taking an annual physical exam. It doesn't mean there is a problem in your relationship, but it may prevent one from forming. And certainly, if there are long-standing areas of bitterness, hurt, or resentment between the partners, marriage counseling may be the only thing that can help.

Returning To Rose-Colored Glasses

When you first fall in love, you focus solely on your partner's good qualities. You notice how clever or witty your partner is, and you appreciate and respect your partner's hopes, dreams, and aspirations. As long as you focus on the positive, you're sure to find it. In the beginning, you project all your fantasies of the ideal lover onto your new partner. You imagine your partner to be a supremely virtuous person who will only enhance your life, and who will never hurt or abandon you. These fantasies create the "highs" of new love.

Problems arise when you realize that your new partner doesn't always match your fantasy ideals. Everyone has human frailties, of course. And everyone has bad days, when they may inadvertently say something hurtful or unkind. When your new partner inevitably pierces your fantasy bubble, you think, "Oh no, this isn't my dream lover after all!" You also fear being hurt by this person.

This is when you begin looking at your partner with a critical eye. Once you start to look for problems or negative traits, you're sure to find them. The critical eye influences everything you see in your once-perfect partner. The sense of humor you once marveled at you now view as "immaturity." The marvelous goals and aspirations of the other person become evidence that she is "nothing but a dreamer." Where once you thought of your partner as sweet, you now think of him as "weak."

Your partner is still the same person. You are just viewing him or her from a different perspective.

Recapturing the good feelings of new love requires you, once again, to cover your critical eyes with rose-colored glasses. The following exercise will help.

Think about your partner for a moment, and try to remember the time you fell in love. Ask yourself: *What did I find attractive in my partner?* Write or make a mental list of the five things that most attracted you to your partner. They can be physical characteristics or personality traits.

The Qualities I Was Initially Most Attracted To In My Partner

1. _____

2. _____

3. _____

4. _____

Make a list of at least five things with which you fell in love. If you can list more than five, even better. If writing this list makes you feel a little sad, this is a normal response. You may be grieving the loss of your idealized vision of your mate. You had hoped for a great love relationship, and this hope died. All deaths trigger grieving responses. If you feel this type of sadness in you, writing about it in a private "feelings journal" is an effective and ideal way to understand and to lessen the emotional pain.

Keep the list of five characteristics with you, either mentally or physically. The next time you are with your partner, focus on finding these five characteristics. They still exist in your partner, and if you look closely, you are certain to rediscover them.

Here are some bad habits that reinforce keeping a negative and critical eye on a love partner. If you engage in these habits, it's important to realize how they can damage your relationship:

1. Swapping "horror stories" with your friends. This involves talking about the negative traits and behaviors of your love partner. The friend listens sympathetically to how bad your relationship is, thus reinforcing your view that your partner—and your partnership—is defective.

2. Reading "Relationship Quiz" articles in magazines. These quizzes, purporting to analyze your love partner and your relationship, are rarely prepared using the scientific method. The quiz authors are often unqualified lay-people and the quiz contains overly-generalized questions and result implications. These quizzes can be entertaining, and some may contain kernels of wisdom and useful information; but be careful not to base your opinion of your partner and your relationship solely on such quiz results.

3. Projecting your own relationship onto the talk show circuit. Daytime talk shows, featuring psychologists and guests discussing common human problems, are entertaining and often informative. They are sincere efforts to teach audiences about living a better life. But frequent-talk show watchers can fall into a dangerous habit: They project themselves and their partners into all the shows. For example, Sylvia watched a talk show about husbands who sleep with their secretaries. All of a sudden, Sylvia was convinced that her husband was cheating on her. He wasn't; he was a very devoted husband. But Sylvia was projecting her insecurities onto the talk show topics.

Be careful of these traps. You don't want an overly-critical eye. No one wants to be a naive fool, and no one wants to be in an unsatisfying love relationship, but it's a positive step to search for the good qualities in your love partner. If you look for the good, you're sure to find it.

Once you rediscover these positive qualities, be sure to acknowledge them. Reward your partner with compliments, kisses, and caresses. Let your partner know that you appreciate these good characteristics, and they're more likely to be reinforced and repeated.

Make the first move and give generous praise. If you're in a relationship that has lacked compliments for some time, your partner may be confused or even threatened by your changed behavior. As a result, you may not get a loving response in return. Keep it up, though, because every human being craves warmth, sincerity, love, kindness, and appreciation. It's what we all live for. Your partner will soon warm up to your praise and will reciprocate in full.

The Best of Both Worlds

Sometimes, our memories have holes in them. We think back fondly to the "good old days," and forget that there were moments that were less than perfect. Psychologists call this inclination "euphoric recall"—the tendency to color our memories of the past with overly-rosy images.

Euphoric recall interferes with accurate memories of our newly-in-love days.

Yes, the first blush of love feels wonderful. But one of the reasons for the "high" associated with romantic love is the uncertainty attached to it—the "he loves me, he loves me not" syndrome. Before the new relationship is cemented into a commitment, there are a million doubts attached to it. We worry that the relationship won't work out:

♥ Will she think I'm boring?

♥ Will he like my outfit?

♥ Will she meet another guy before I have a chance to prove myself?

♥ Will he be more attracted to another woman?

We also worry that the relationship will work out:

♥ What if she wants to get married?

♥ What if he wants me to move in with him?

♥ What if he wants to go to bed right away?

New love can be awfully stressful!

The great thing about lasting love is that you can intertwine the highs of new love with the highs of long-term love, if you make the effort.

The highs of new love come from feeling loved and appreciated by this new person in your life. The highs also stem from the abundance of affection poured on you by your new lover. You feel strong, like you've risen above all your cares or worries. New love makes you feel this way because your partner gives you so much positive feedback. Your new lover is generous with praise.

The highs of long-term love come from different sources: the security of knowing you'll always have a date on Saturday night, the ready availability of a monogamous sex partner (who already knows what you like sexually!), and shared memories and experiences. And, for those who apply, the joys of parenthood.

You can have the best of both worlds—new love and long-term love—by combining a steady supply of praise and compliments with lots of affection, passion, and sex. Give, and you will receive.

Chapter Eight
Courting Your Mate

"Just getting out of the house alone with my wife is roman-
tic. It's great when we drop the kids off at Grandma's house
and the two of us just head out for an evening alone
together."   —39-year-old r. arried man

When you think of "dating," what comes to mind? Young
couples at restaurants or in movie theaters? New lovers
walking hand in hand in the park? What about married

lovers? Do married couples date each other? Is a love life possible after you've had children?

Too often, after a couple moves in together, they stop dating. And when two people stop dating, it is very easy to forget to acknowledge each other romantically. Romance is replaced with day-to-day chores, career duties, and routine sex. At the most, passion consists of a kiss or a hug.

Wendy and Terry were married for 11 years and had three young children. They were both active members of their church and both held management positions that kept them busy at least 50 hours every week. When they came home from work, the kids needed help with homework, sports practice, or music lessons. The couple's only time alone together happened around 10 o'clock, when the kids were finally asleep.

Sex was fairly routine, with Terry on top. It never occurred to either partner to try different sexual positions. Both were too tired to think about it.

Couples like Terry and Wendy, who are sleep-walking through their sex lives, can benefit greatly from reinfusing energy into their relationship. As hard as it seems, there is a way to balance responsibilities so that the children, career, and housework are taken care of, without sacrificing love and passion.

When you think about it, the love relationship is your reason for working and having children, isn't it? You married out of love. You had children because you were in love with your partner. You built a home and a life around this person.

Unfortunately, it's too easy to lose sight of the central importance of this relationship. And it's extremely easy to postpone putting energy into your love life. There are too many, seemingly more urgent, responsibilities vying for your immediate attention.

Date Night

I've discovered, when working with couples like Terry and Wendy, that both partners are anxious to have a fun, happy relationship. Neither partner wants a routine, overly-responsible life that is devoid of great sex or passionate romance. Usually, however, both partners feel that the other person should do something to improve the situation.

Since both partners feel overwhelmed by their day-to-day responsibilities, they resent the "obligation" to create romance in the relationship. "Don't I do enough already?" is the angry thought accompanying this dilemma. So, they wait for their partner to pull a romantic trick out of his or her hat.

As a psychotherapist, I've learned that the best solution to this common impasse is to assign a weekly "Date Night" to couples. This means that they choose a night, say Thursday or Saturday, to be their official "date night." Every week, they must go out of the house alone (read: no children or friends) and have a date! Now, the date usually involves dinner or a concert or a movie, or any other activity that the couple may want to do. The "what" of the date is unimportant. What *is* important is that the couple is spending uninterrupted time together. Alone.

Every couple needs to date, regardless of how long they've been together. Just like an exercise program, which takes effort and planning but which yields tremendous benefits, a weekly date ensures that your love will stay healthy and vital.

The ideal arrangement is for couples to agree jointly on a regular night for the date, and then alternate planning for the date. That way, each partner is responsible for two dates per month. When arranging your date nights, the most important thing is this: *No matter what, you must not break the date.* The date must take priority over every other thing that could possibly come up, except perhaps if one partner is seriously ill or injured. Even then, arrange the date in the hospital or at your partner's bedside.

If you put the date into a "must" category, you're more likely to come up with creative means for executing your plans. Many couples say, "We can't afford to go out. Restaurants and movies are too expensive, and baby-sitters cost a fortune!" I say this is an excuse, or an indication that the couple's priorities have shifted away from the love relationship. Everybody has room in their budgets to cut something out. Cut down on the amount you spend in another area and divert that money to your date nights. Think of the dates not as a luxury, but as a necessity.

The dates don't need to cost a lot of money to be effective. You can go to a matinee movie at 6:00 and save enough money to cover the cost of two glasses of wine at dinner. Skip the valet parking at the restaurant and you'll have extra money for dessert. Arrange cooperative baby-sitting exchanges with friends or another couple from church, school, or work, and you'll save a fortune in childcare costs.

If you take only one step toward improving your love life, this must be it. Nothing else is as important. Regular dates are a breath of fresh air that remind you that you're a couple in love. Just make sure that the dates remove you from your regular routine, because that's what makes them special.

Opal and Jerome eat at restaurants constantly, because their hectic work schedules made shopping for food and preparing meals difficult. For them, a date night should not consist *solely* of dinner in a restaurant. It needs to include a special walk together, or a movie, or other event. Dating needs to remove you and your partner from the routines of day-to-day living.

Here are some romantic ideas for dates with your partner. You can get other ideas by reading the "Bulletin Board" or "Activities" section in your newspaper.

Have fun, and make them as elaborate as your financial budget allows!

Inexpensive Dates

♥ Going to a local resort hotel and walking around the grounds and the lobby

♥ Preparing a romantic picnic and heading to a park

♥ Going window-shopping

♥ Going on a long bicycle ride together

♥ Going to a museum or an art gallery

♥ Seeing a matinee movie

♥ Having coffee and dessert at an inexpensive coffee shop

♥ Going to a drive-in movie

♥ Renting roller-skates

♥ Test-driving a car

♥ Attending an arts and crafts festival

♥ Flying kites

♥ Watching a high school sports game

♥ Being in the studio audience of a local television show.

Moderately Expensive Dates

- ♥ Renting a convertible and going for a long drive
- ♥ Go to a wine-tasting or food-festival event
- ♥ Listening to music over drinks
- ♥ Going to a bookstore and buying each other a book to read
- ♥ Dining at a restaurant you've never tried before
- ♥ Dancing at a nightclub
- ♥ Attending a professional sporting event
- ♥ Going to a comedy club
- ♥ Going to a local amusement park without your children (this will really make you feel like a kid again!)
- ♥ Having portrait photos taken of just the two of you together
- ♥ Attending a local play.

Expensive Dates

- ♥ Renting a limousine for the evening
- ♥ Flying out of town just for dinner or a quick overnight trip
- ♥ Attending the opera, symphony, concert, or ballet
- ♥ Reserving a really great hotel room for the evening

♥ Going on a dinner cruise on a boat or a train

♥ Shopping for a big-ticket present for yourselves (a new television or stereo, for example).

Chapter Nine

Backrubs and Bubblebaths

*"When my wife massages me all over, I get so relaxed it's
like I'm melting. Then, she turns me over and starts rubbing
my chest. By the time she gets to my genitals, I'm already
so turned on that I practically explode when she takes me in
her hands."* —47-year-old married
man

Before sexual arousal can occur, the body must be relaxed. This may sound ironic, but it's true. Think of it this
way: If you're worried, distracted, stressed, or tense,
you'll have a difficult time achieving an orgasm. On the

other hand, if you're too relaxed from alcohol, drugs, or fatigue, you'll also have trouble getting aroused.

In fact, a study appearing in the *New England Journal of Medicine* found that the most frequent sexual difficulty reported by women was "an inability to relax." Fully 47 percent of the women surveyed complained that this difficulty in relaxing was the biggest factor blocking their sexual pleasure and fulfillment. Twelve percent of the men also said that they had trouble relaxing enough to enjoy sex.

The central nervous system (our spinal cord and brain) controls the body's sexual arousal process. There are two parts to the central nervous system: the sympathetic, which controls alertness, and the parasympathetic, which controls relaxation. Think of a *para*chute floating calmly to the ground and you'll never forget that the *para*sympathetic nervous system controls relaxation. The sympathetic nervous system goes into effect when we're stressed or in danger—for example, when we're driving in heavy stop-and-go traffic. Only one system is on at a time.

The parasympathetic nervous system, the relaxing one, is responsible for sexual arousal and orgasm. So, if you're tense or worried, you won't be turned on. If your thoughts are centered on problems at work, or fears about pleasing your partner, your sympathetic nervous system will kick in. And believe me, the sympathetic nervous system is not very sympathetic to your desire for sex!

Mona and Kevin had frustrating experiences because their tensions distracted them from having enjoyable sex. Mona could only orgasm when alone and masturbating by herself. Whenever she tried to make herself come with Kevin, she would become self-conscious and lose her sexual concentration.

"It's no use," Mona told me. "If I use a vibrator in front of Kevin, I'm embarrassed about how I must look. I think my face must be contorting or my stomach sagging or sticking out. So Kevin will try to make me come using his hand or his mouth. But the trouble is, I'll worry whether Kevin is getting tired or sore. I worry I'm taking too long to have an orgasm, and then I end up not having one at all! Sometimes, I'll fake it just to get the whole thing over with."

Another couple, Kent and Beverly, had also had sexual difficulties due to tension. During their 10-year marriage, Kent and Beverly had always enjoyed lovemaking. But one evening, Kent had difficulty maintaining an erection. Both partners were upset; Kent because his penis wouldn't cooperate, and Beverly because she assumed that the problem was *her*.

This created a negative cycle, because the next time the couple went to make love, Kent was afraid of losing his erection. Beverly was afraid, too—afraid that she was losing her attractiveness. With both partners feeling tense and pressured, it was virtually guaranteed that their fears would be self-fulfilling. Kent had difficulty even getting an erection.

When it was evident that he wasn't going to become physically aroused, Kent suggested at least taking care of Beverly's pleasure through oral sex. But because Beverly suddenly felt unattractive, she was too distracted to concentrate on enjoying the oral sex. Both went to sleep frustrated.

Serotonin— the Sexual Brain Chemical

Caffeine. Alcohol. Fatigue. Illness. Drugs. Worries. Self-consciousness. All can spoil an otherwise-perfect setting for romance and sexual pleasure. Being too relaxed is just as bad for sexual arousal as being too tense.

The central nervous system is fueled by chemicals called "neurotransmitters," which are liquid messengers that influence mood and energy levels. These chemicals in the brain are like chlorine in a pool—they must be in correct balance and proportion or the environment (the body or the pool) suffers.

One chemical in particular plays a dramatic part in influencing energy levels, moods, and sexual arousal. This brain chemical is called "serotonin." You've probably heard of it, because this neurotransmitter is an important player in many bodily functions such as appetite, PMS, and sleep quality.

Serotonin is produced by the brain during REM, or "rapid eye movement" sleep, which is the dreaming period of our sleeping cycle. The body can't store serotonin, so it must produce a fresh supply every night. If you don't produce enough serotonin, you'll wake up feeling sleepy and won't be in an optimum mood. You may even feel depressed or irritable when your serotonin level is too low. If you have an oversupply of serotonin, you'll feel edgy, uptight, or tense.

Many factors affect serotonin production. If you don't get enough REM sleep, you won't produce enough serotonin. REM sleep is reduced when you drink alcohol excessively or abuse depressant drugs, including valium. Insomnia, of course, interferes with the entire sleep cycle. So if you can't sleep because you're worried or have had too much caffeine, you won't get enough REM sleep or serotonin.

After a night of heavy drinking or fitful sleeping, you feel groggy, confused, and irritable. This "hangover" is the result of insufficient serotonin. The body then attempts to compensate by requiring you to eat something that will produce serotonin—namely, carbohydrates. When you are hung-over from overdrinking or a lack of sleep, you'll notice that you crave foods like bread, cereal, crackers, ice cream, chocolate, candy, cake, or pie. These foods are all high in carbohydrates that increase the amount of serotonin in your brain, and provide a blood-glucose boost that stimulates energy levels.

Women may notice that they crave these foods right before their menstrual cycles. This is because serotonin is depleted immediately before menstruation, and many pre-menstrual syndrome (PMS) symptoms stem from inadequate serotonin levels. The hormonal shifts accompanying menstruation deplete serotonin and create PMS symptoms like irritability and fatigue.

Low serotonin levels also lead to lowered sexual energy and pleasure. Sexual arousal and orgasm are contingent on a sufficient supply of serotonin. If a person's serotonin level is low, then so is his or her energy level. When a person's serotonin level is low, he or she becomes irritable. This puts the person into the sympathetic nervous system, and blocks sexual arousal and orgasm. Studies show that serotonin depletion interferes with orgasm.

In Chapters Ten and Eleven, we'll look at food's role in creating a romantic climate. It isn't just the candlelights, soft music, and beauty of the meal that leads to lovemaking after dinner. The chemical properties that make up the food—carbohydrates, proteins, amino acids, and other components—affect serotonin and other brain chemistries. And that, in turn, affects sexual arousal.

Slipping Into Something More Comfortable

Now that we've covered the basic physiology leading to sexual arousal, it's time to put that knowledge into action.

You and your partner will enjoy lovemaking when you are both in an optimum state of relaxation. As we've seen, too much relaxation and too much tension interfere with sexual arousal and orgasm. Romance and passion are hinged on being relaxed and having a fun time.

Relaxing with your love partner is as important to foreplay as kissing. The couple desiring romance and passion can help each other unwind after a tense day of working, commuting, negotiating, or parenting. Here are some suggestions:

♥ Taking a brief nap after arriving home from work

♥ Bathing and changing into comfortable clothing

♥ Taking turns giving each other backrubs and massages

♥ Taking a long walk or a bicycle ride together

♥ Turning off the telephone and ignoring the doorbell

♥ Waiting until later to open the mail (especially bills!)

♥ Sitting in a hot tub or a jacuzzi together

♥ Taking a bubble bath together, complete with candles and champagne or ginger ale

♥ Arranging a baby-sitter for the children, or arranging an activity that keeps the children busy or quiet

♥ Making an agreement not to argue with each other, no matter what!

♥ Taking a long, scenic drive in the countryside

♥ Renting a favorite movie (especially a comedy, since laughter is relaxing)

♥ Lying down together in an embrace.

A Touch of Relaxation

When your days are hectic and you and your parter are off leading your separate lives, it's easy to lose touch with each other. Sure, you may catch up briefly during dinner, but you need more to feel truly close to your partner. You need to reconnect with each other regularly.

Touch is an essential component of staying close to your partner. Emotional closeness accompanies physical closeness. There are some studies suggesting that smelling each other triggers a sense of closeness to your partner. The studies on "pheromones," the below-conscious-awareness-level smells we all carry, indicate that the chemical attraction we feel may happen because of pheromones.

The theory is that pheromones work like locks and keys. Each smell, including a pheromone, has a molecular shape. Our olfactory system (the scientific term for our sense of smell) has spaces that recognize certain odors. Smells are like keys fitting into locks in our olfactory system. When we meet a person whose pheromones fit into our olfactory "locks," we are attracted to that person. If he or she fits our other criteria as a suitable romantic partner, we call this pheromone attraction "love."

The pheromone theory continues that we can get a "high" off our partner's pheromones that is addictive. The theorists speculate that this is why it is difficult to break away from an unhealthy relationship. We are addicted to the other person's chemistry, even if that person is abusive or unfaithful.

Now, this may appear to be a less than romantic theory about attraction, but I believe that there's a great deal of validity to it. I strongly believe that when we touch each other we reconnect partly because of pheromone exchanges. I think this is one reason we feel so close to our partner after making love.

Non-sexual touch is as vital as sexual touch to a healthy relationship. If we limit our physical contact to sexual intercourse, we miss out on simple pleasures that actually add to sexual enjoyment. In fact, couples experiencing sexual difficulties are counseled to engage exclusively in non-sexual touch as a way of "sensitizing" their bodies to the pleasures of flesh on flesh. If our only physical contact is sexual, we can easily become numbed to subtle physical sensations—and this numbing can seriously limit sexual pleasure.

Here are some non-sexual touching exercises you may find pleasurable, as well as helpful:

♥ Slowly stroke your partner's hair. Feel how the different strands have different textures. Notice how your partner relaxes when you massage his or her head. Firmly massage the neck muscles in a rhythmic fashion.

♥ Rub your thumb around your partner's palm. Twirl the thumb softly in circles, as though to tickle the underside of his or her hand. Touch each finger by running your thumb up and down each side. Concentrate your attention on the details of your partner's hand.

♥ Pretend that you're on a first date with your partner, and that you're touching each other for the first time. Focus your attention on your partner's skin texture and bone structure. Run your hand slowly across your partner's shoulders and arms.

♥ Exchange deep muscle massages with each other. Take your time and avoid rushing as you knead your partner's muscles.

♥ While watching television together, sit facing each other so that you can exchange foot rubs. Rub your partner's foot deeply, especially concentrating on the ball of the foot. Enjoy it as your partner rubs your foot simultaneously.

Chapter Ten
Enchanting, Arousing Mealtimes

"To me, the most romantic thing a woman can do is to make an effort. If she fixes a candlelight dinner and we enjoy it with wine next to the fireplace, there's nothing better. To me, romance and love take effort, and that effort is definitely worth it!" —33-year-old single man

In the survey I conducted examining opinions about romance, most men and women listed dinner as a setting leading to romantic feelings. Many people also mentioned candlelight and soft music as an important accompaniment to dinner's romantic ambience.

It's no accident that so many people view dinner as a romantic step toward an evening of love and passion. Dinner fulfills many ingredients necessary to romance:

♥ It provides an opportunity to relax. Dinner marks the transition point between daytime—which is usually busy and full of responsibilities—and evening.

♥ Dinner brings you physically close to your partner, allowing you time to exchange conversation. This constitutes a warm-up period and allows you to reconnect with your spouse or your lover.

♥ The mood-altering chemicals in many dinner combinations triggers a resupply of the brain chemical serotonin, and helps refuel the body and blood sugar level. (In the previous chapter, we discussed the role serotonin plays in mood, energy level, sexual arousa, and orgasm.)

Sexy Food Combinations

Serotonin is produced in greater quantities when a certain food combination is eaten. Studies conducted around the globe—including the Massachusetts Institute of Technology, the University of Leeds (United Kingdom), the National Institute of Neurological Diseases and Stroke in Maryland, Rockefeller University in New York, Tel Aviv University and Medical Center (Israel), the University of Cagliari (Italy), the University of Uppsala (Sweden), the University Claude Bernard School of Medicine (France), and the University of Bern (Switzerland)—have discovered links between serotonin production and dietary ingredients.

Consistently, studies show that carbohydrates are necessary for the brain to manufacture sufficient serotonin. Further studies by Richard and Judith Wurtman of M.I.T. also linked foods high in the amino acid tryptophan with serotonin production.

The Wurtmans' extensive research concludes that optimum serotonin production occurs when carbohydrates are eaten with a tryptophan source. Tryptophan, at one time, was available in supplemental pill forms. Unfortunately, a Japanese vitamin manufacturer with unsanitary practices produced contaminated tryptophan pills. These contaminated l-tryptophan supplements were labeled and distributed through American sources, and resulted in several deaths and serious illnesses. Instead of controlling vitamin importation standards, the FDA and CDC decided to ban tryptophan distribution altogether.

Tryptophan is nothing more than an amino acid naturally occurring in many foods. Most protein sources are rich in tryptophan, including beef, chicken, turkey, and many seafoods.

Tryptophan's mood-altering properties occur because it triggers serotonin production. Tryptophan ingestion, and the accompanying serotonin creation, create feelings of peace and calm. Too much serotonin, however, can make you feel sleepy. Too little serotonin has the same effect. The optimum serotonin level creates a "just right" feeling. Kind of like the story of Goldilocks looking for the perfect bed to sleep in, isn't it?

According to the Wurtmans' research, when a food high in tryptophan is combined with a carbohydrate, the brain's serotonin production is increased. Tryptophan is a catalyst—also known as a "precursor"—for serotonin production. But the tryptophan first must penetrate a part of the brain called the "blood brain barrier." The carbohydrate helps the tryptophan cross this barrier.

What does this mean for you, in search of a romantic dinner menu? It means that the perfect meal combines one of the following high-tryptophan ingredients with a carbohydrate:

Foods High In Tryptophan (in Milligrams)

Dairy Products

Cottage cheese, 1 cup, 1% fat	312
Cottage cheese, 1 cup, 2% fat	346
Ice Cream, 1 cup, vanilla	100
Milk, 1 cup, lowfat or whole	113
Milk, 1 cup, nonfat	118
Parmesan cheese, 1 ounce	137
Swiss cheese, 1 ounce	114

Fish and Shellfish (all are cooked, 3 1/2 ounce portions):

Bass	231
Cod	260
Haddock	196
Halibut	315
Lobster	152
Mackerel	283
Pompano	229
Salmon	270
Shrimp	242
Tuna	247

Beef (all are cooked portions)

Hamburger, 1 patty, 85 grams, lean	303

Porterhouse steak, 100 grams, lean	297
Round steak, top portion, 111 grams, lean	504
Sirloin steak, 125 grams, lean	373
T-bone steak, 95 grams, lean	281

Lamb (all are cooked portions)

Blade chop, 1 lean, 93 grams	329
Loin chop, 3 1/2 ounce	298
Rib chop, lean, 3 1/2 ounce	263

Pork (all are cooked portions)

Bacon, Canadian, approximately 3 slices, 63 grams	180
Bacon, cured, 5 slices (6 grams each)	95
Blade steak, 3 1/2 ounces	323
Ham, 3 1/2 ounces	427
Loin chop, 3 1/2 ounces	382
Sausage, 5 links (13 grams each)	100
Sausage, 2 patties (27 grams each)	84
Spareribs, 6 medium (90 grams total)	198
Tenderloin, 3 1/2 ounces	398

Poultry (all are cooked portions)

Chicken Breast, 1/2 (86 grams), without skin	311
Chicken Drumstick, 2 (88 grams) without skin	290
Chicken Thigh, 2 (102 grams total), without skin	316
Duck, 100 grams (3.5 ounces), without skin	327

| Turkey Dark Meat, 100 grams (3.5 ounces), without skin | 325 |
| Turkey Light Meat, 100 grams (3.5 ounces) without skin | 340 |

Nuts

Cashews, roasted (50 grams), 20-25 nuts	215
Mixed nuts (50 grams)	236
Peanuts, roasted without skin (50 grams)	196
Pumpkin Seeds (50 grams)	261
Sesame Seeds (50 grams)	241
Sunflower Seeds (50 grams)	180

These high-tryptophan foods, when combined with ingredients high in carbohydrates, propel the production of serotonin. In addition, carbohydrates provide fuel for energy. What a delicious combination for passion: energy plus a wonderful feeling of calm and tranquility! This combination is possible with the help of a meal combining tryptophan with carbohydrates.

High-carbohydrate foods are based on glucose, a sugar component. The major carbohydrate categories are breads and fruits. Grains, breads, pastas, flour, and cereal are all high in carbohydrates. Fruits, whether fresh, canned, juiced, or dried are also loaded with carbohydrates.

This means that a dinner combining a bread product with one of the high-tryptophan ingredients listed above, is the optimum combination for your dinner dates. The possibilities are endless: pasta with seafood, beef or poultry, especially when topped with cheese. Pizza is another good choice, as are Mexican foods combining tortillas with meat and cheese.

To me, it's fascinating that foods from the "romantic countries"—Italy, France, Spain—are based on the carbohydrate-tryptophan combination. Foods from less emotionally-expressive countries usually don't have this specific combination.

The recipes listed below lend themselves to romantic evenings. I've included a variety of menus, from elaborate to quick and easy. When planning your romantic dinner, the most important ingredient is *you*. Fixing dinner should be pleasant, not a chore that you resent. The pace of the evening needs to be relaxed, yet upbeat. Don't worry about everything being "perfect," because when something inevitably happens—the food gets overcooked or you run out of a certain ingredient—you'll lose the relaxation integral to passion and sexual arousal.

Have fun with dinner. Whether you cook together or alone, think of it as an adventure or an experiment. Allow your mind to wander, and daydream as you cook away (but be careful to not let things burn as you allow yourself to fantasize).

Here are some ways to spice up your dinner preparation:

♥ Make an agreement with your partner to take turns preparing dinner. Fixing a meal is a symbolic way of showing love and care. You are literally providing for the other person's welfare when you serve them a meal, and this speaks to our most basic needs. It triggers deep feelings of appreciation and love.

♥ Have fun cooking together, and make it a game of play. Don't compete with each other to see who is the best chef, because this competition will lead to anxiety or to anger. If your partner makes a suggestion in the kitchen, try to see it for what it is—a suggestion—and not as a personal criticism. If, however, there is friction whenever the two of you cook together, you'll need to make other arrangements. Either take turns cooking on different evenings, or discuss which roles each of you will play while preparing the meal.

♥ While cooking, dress in a provocative outfit—whether you're a man or a woman. Try cooking in just an apron, or if you're a woman, try it in high heels and lingerie. Just as you pre-heat an oven, you'll be preparing your own mood for later in the evening.

♥ Make dinner a leisurely, unhurried affair. Light the candles, turn on the soft music (not the radio, however, because commercials may spoil the mood).

♥ Serve hors d'oeuvres.

♥ Don't eat so much dinner that you're stuffed, or so little that you remain hungry. Either way will leave you out of the mood.

♥ If any disagreement, tension, conflict or argument arises, avoid pursuing it this evening. Of course, you don't want to stuff down intense feelings of anger. But you don't need to try resolving problems in your relationship every evening. Take a break tonight and promise yourself you won't indulge in taking offense to your partner's words or actions. If you can't go one evening without arguing, then marriage counseling may be in order. One way to forgo arguing is to resolve, "I won't fight back." It takes two to argue, and you can be the one who remains in control. For many couples, arguing is an ingrained habit of communicating. This habit was learned, and can be unlearned.

♥ If it helps, pretend that you're on a first date with your partner. Imagine that everything's fresh and new, and wipe your mental slate clean. This thought alone may enliven your mood and your energy level.

♥ Take the time today to learn a new joke, and share it with your partner during dinner.

♥ Try feeding each other. It's fun and sexy!

♥ Take the time to savor every bite of your meal. You'll eat more slowly, and won't be as likely to stuff yourself.

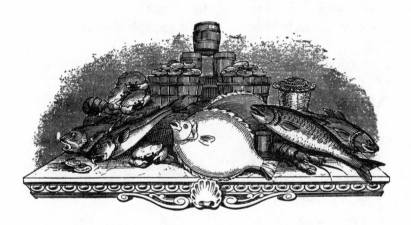

Passionate Dinner Menus

Salmon Mousse Manicotti

This sexy dinner is as beautiful as it is delicious. The recipe makes enough for two dinners, and the leftovers are just as delightful as the first serving.

Salmon mousse filling
3/4 pound salmon fillet, de-boned
1 Tablespoon butter or margarine
1 container ricotta cheese (15 ounces)
12 ounces shredded mozzarella cheese
3/4 cup grated (not powdered) Parmesan cheese
1 egg
1/8 teaspoon salt
1/4 teaspoon pepper
Optional: 1/4 cup crushed walnuts

White sauce
1 Tablespoon butter or margarine (not low-calorie)
1/2 teaspoon ground or crushed garlic
1/2 cup sliced mushrooms
16 ounces sour cream
6 1/2 ounce can of minced clams with juice
1/4 cup crumbled feta cheese

Pasta
1 package manicotti (8 ounces)

Dot salmon fillet with butter. Bake salmon in small baking pan in 425 degree oven for 10 minutes. Remove and refrigerate. Reduce oven heat to 375 degrees.

Cook pasta in boiling water with salt and oil, as directed on package. Drain carefully to avoid tearing shells, and set aside in lightly-oiled 13" x 9" baking pan.

Begin white sauce by melting butter over medium heat in large, deep-side skillet. Stir in garlic and sauté 1 minute. Add mushrooms and sauté until mushrooms are soft throughout, about 5 minutes. Blend in sour cream, clams with juice, and feta cheese. Simmer over low heat, stirring as needed.

Meanwhile, in large bowl mix all but 3/4 cup mozzarella cheese with ricotta and Parmesan cheeses. Using hand mixer at medium speed, blend in egg, salt, and pepper until mixture is thoroughly blended and smooth.

Using large fork, separate salmon fillet flesh from skin and any remaining bones. Put pieces into cheese mixture and blend at low speed until entire mixture takes on salmon color and smooth texture. With small spoon scoop mixture into manicotti shells until each is well filled.

Pour white sauce over filled manicotti shells and sprinkle with remaining mozzarella cheese. Bake at 375 degrees for 30 minutes. Turn broiler onto high, and brown cheese topping, taking care not to allow cheese to burn (about 2-3 minutes under broiler should be enough). Serve each person 2-3 manicotti shells, using a spatula to put food onto each plate.

King Crab Alfredo Fettuccine

6 ounces fettuccine noodles
2 King Crab legs, cooked
1/4 cup (1/2 stick) butter
1 cup grated Parmesan cheese
1/2 cup heavy whipping cream

Cook noodles in large pot of boiling water. See package regarding salt and oil. Remove crab meat and place in microwave-safe bowl. Meanwhile, melt butter over medium-low heat, in small saucepan. Slowly stir in 3/4 cup cheese until well blended. Gradually pour in whipping cream, stirring continuously.

Drain noodles into colander and rinse with hot water. Return noodles to cooking pot and pour cream sauce on top. Stir noodles gently until covered with sauce. Heat crab meat in microwave oven for 1 minute at 50 percent power. Serve each plate of noodles with crab meat on top, and sprinkle with remaining Parmesan cheese.

Linguine with Sauteed Shrimp and Clam Marinara Sauce

This flavorful pasta meal is packed with spicy punch. You'll win applause for a sauce that appeals to every bite.

6-8 ounces linguine pasta
2 Tablespoons butter
1 teaspoon crushed garlic
1/4 teaspoon seasoned salt *or* garlic salt *or* onion salt
1 medium-sized brown or Vidalia onion, peeled and
    finely chopped
10 mushrooms, washed and sliced
1 six-ounce can minced or chopped clams
2 six-ounce cans tomato paste, pre-seasoned Italian style
1 eight-ounce can diced tomatoes, pre-seasoned Italian
    style
10 - 15 medium size raw shrimp, peeled and de-veined
3/4 cup grated Parmesan cheese

In large pot, boil water for pasta. See package regarding salt and oil. Cook pasta while preparing marinara sauce.

Melt butter in deep skillet over medium heat. Stir in garlic and seasoned salt. Sauté onions until transparent and slightly browned. Add mushrooms and cook until very tender. Stir in clams, including juice, and blend in tomato paste and tomatoes. Add 1/4 cup Parmesan cheese.

When sauce is very hot and cheese is melted, and linguine is cooked enough, add shrimp to marinara sauce. Gently fold in shrimp and stir continuously until shrimp is pink on both sides.

Immediately drain linguine and rinse with hot water. Serve pasta on plate and spoon marinara sauce and shrimp over pasta. Sprinkle remaining Parmesan cheese on each plate.

Turkey Wellington

This takeoff on the traditional Beef Wellington dish is a healthy alternative for couples who want to eat light yet still enjoy a gourmet treat.

1 package phyllo dough (available in the freezer section of the grocery store)
1 pound turkey, light or dark meat
8 ounces mushrooms, sliced
4 Tablespoons butter
2 teaspoons seasoned salt
1 egg, beaten

Preheat oven to 350 degrees (F).

Bake turkey, mushrooms, 2 Tablespoons butter, and 1 teaspoon seasoned salt in foil-covered pan for 15 minutes. Remove from oven and refrigerate turkey and mushrooms for an additional 15 minutes.

Melt remaining butter on low heat or in the microwave oven. Stir in remaining seasoned salt. Spread 1 sheet of phyllo dough on cutting board and brush it completely, but lightly, with butter mixture. Add another phyllo dough sheet on top of the first and brush it, too, with butter. Repeat until you have stacked and butter-brushed six phyllo dough sheets.

Put 1/4 turkey and mushrooms on top, and in center, of phyllo dough stack. Roll dough around turkey. Continue process until you have made 4 turkey-and-phyllo-dough rolls. Place rolls in a buttered pan and brush all rolls with beaten egg to give them a glaze.

Bake turkey rolls at 350 degrees, in center of the oven, for 20 minutes or until they turn golden brown.

Creamy Chicken Crêpes

These crêpes rival any you'd eat at a fancy French restaurant. The secret is in watching the crêpes to ensure they don't overcook. If you've never made them before, you may need to cook one or two before feeling completely comfortable with the process. Once you've mastered the "wrist action" involved, you'll cook crêpes like a master French chef!

Cook's Note: The crêpe batter needs to be prepared and refrigerated approximately 2 hours before you plan to cook dinner. A crêpe pan is helpful in making this dish, but a small rounded non-stick frying pan will do.

Crêpes
2 eggs
2/3 cup milk
1 Tablespoon oil
1/2 cup all-purpose flour
1/4 teaspoon salt

Beat eggs in medium bowl. Stir in milk and oil. Gradually stir in flour and salt and beat until mixture is smooth. Cover batter and refrigerate 2 hours.
Meanwhile, prepare Chicken Filling.

Chicken Filling
When ready to cook, lightly brush crêpe or frying pan with oil and heat until hot. Stir batter. Add 4 Tablespoons of batter to hot pan and tilt pan quickly so batter runs and covers entire surface, creating a round circle. Turn crêpe carefully with large spatula, when bubbles begin to form in center and underside is golden brown.

Fill each crêpe with the Chicken Filling and roll each side closed. Cover filled crêpes with remaining Chicken Filling and sprinkle grated cheese over top. Broil crêpes and cheese briefly to brown cheese.

Chicken Sauce

1 chicken breast (2 halves) skinned and diced into 1-inch
    cubes or pieces
2 Tablespoons butter
2 Tablespoons onion, finely chopped
1 can condensed cream of chicken soup
10 medium mushrooms, washed and sliced
1/2 cup milk
1/2 cup sour cream
1/4 teaspoon paprika
1/8 teaspoon salt
1/8 teaspoon pepper
1/2 cup jack or mozzarella cheese, finely grated

In deep frying pan, melt butter over medium heat. Sauté onions until they are transparent. Add mushrooms and heat until they are brown and tender. Add chicken meat and stir until chicken is white throughout. Add soup and milk and heat until all are blended. Stir in sour cream and spices, setting cheese aside for topping filled crêpes.

Chicken and Mushroom Crescents with Cheese

This is a quick-and-easy meal that is both exotic and elegant. You will probably adopt it as a regular treat in your household because of its easy preparation and its delicious taste.

2 chicken breast halves, skinned
3 Tablespoons butter
8 ounces mushrooms, sliced
2 teaspoons seasoned salt
2 packages pre-made crescent rolls, 8 crescents per
    package
1 cup finely grated cheddar or jack cheese
1 egg, beaten

Preheat oven to 425 degrees.

Place chicken breasts, butter, seasoned salt, and mushrooms in small baking pan and cover with aluminum foil. Bake 15 minutes, or until chicken meat turns completely white. Remove to refrigerator.

Meanwhile, open crescent roll packages onto large cutting board. Place 3 triangles together and push edges together, until they are fused into a single, big triangle. You'll have 5 big triangles, with 1 small triangle left over.

Remove chicken and mushrooms from refrigerator and tear or cut into small pieces. Fill each crescent triangle evenly with chicken, mushrooms, and cheese and roll into traditional crescent shape.

Place filled crescents on ungreased cookie sheet and brush lightly with beaten egg. Bake 10-12 minutes, or until crescents are even, golden brown.

Double-Stuffed Pizza

This is a delicious treat that puts home-delivered commercial pizzas to shame. You'll love the taste, and if you serve it with a fresh side salad, the meal is actually as healthy as it is tantalizing.

Cook's Note: Before attempting to cook your own pizza, it's a good idea to invest in a quality pizza pan. A bad pizza pan usually results in burned or unevenly cooked crusts. I use a vented pan that has never failed to deliver fabulous pizza crusts.

Pizza Crust
3 cups all-purpose flour
1 package active dry yeast (not the quick variety)
1/2 teaspoon salt
1 cup hot water
2 Tablespoons virgin olive oil
1 egg

Combine 1 1/2 cups flour, yeast, and salt in large bowl that you can later cover tightly, such as a Tupperware bowl with a sealable top. Slowly add water and oil and beat 2 minutes at medium speed. Add egg and mix an additional minute. Slowly add 1/2 cup additional flour and beat another minute, still at medium speed. Turn beater to high speed and slowly add 3/4 cup to 1 cup more flour until mixture turns into a soft dough. Take dough out of bowl and place on lightly-floured surface. Knead vigorously and steadily for 5 minutes. Return dough to bowl and cover tightly. Set aside in warm or room-temperature location to let it rise approximately 30 minutes, while you prepare toppings.

Toppings

2 small (6 ounce) cans tomato paste, pre-mixed with Italian seasonings such as oregano, basil, thyme and garlic
2 1/2 cups grated mixed cheese, consisting of mozzarella, Parmesan and provolone (mozzarella alone does not have enough flavor)
1/2 pound ground lean turkey
5 - 8 mushrooms
2 Tablespoons sliced black olives
1 medium tomato, fresh and chopped
2 teaspoons seasoning salt, onion salt, *or* garlic salt

Separate turkey meat into small pieces in medium frying pan and cook over medium heat. Add 2 teaspoons seasoning salt, onion salt, *or* garlic salt as turkey meat cooks, for flavoring. Drain and set cooked turkey meat aside.

Wash and slice mushrooms and cook in frying pan with leftover juice from turkey, adding small amounts of butter or olive oil if needed. Cook until very tender.

When turkey and mushrooms are cooked, it is time to roll crust. Using floured rolling pin and floured surface, spread crust evenly into round circle 1 inch larger than pizza pan.

Spray pizza pan lightly with nonstick cooking spray and place crust on top. Spread tomato paste over crust and sprinkle with 1 3/4 cups grated cheese. Top with turkey, mushrooms, olives, and tomatoes, and cover with remaining cheese.

Place in center of oven, with cookie sheet on oven shelf below pizza, to catch any wayward melting cheese. Bake at 400 degrees for 25 minutes or until bottom of crust is light golden brown.

Chapter Eleven
Desserts As Foreplay

"There's something about her making me a dessert that puts me in such a great mood. I guess it's the combination of all the trouble she went through and eating something that tastes so good. But, I'll tell you, if you give me dessert I turn into an instant pussycat!"—29-year-old married man

The link between chocolate and romance dates to the days of courtship, when a lovelorn gentleman caller would offer his intended a heart-shaped box of chocolates. Together, they'd sit in the parlor, gaze into each other's eyes, and feed each other one mouth-watering confection after another.

This scenario is no accident, however, because more research is revealing the powerful aphrodisiac qualities inherent in chocolate. Most people have heard by now that chocolate contains the same chemical that the brain creates when we are feeling the delicious emotions of romantic love and infatuation.

Remember feeling lightheaded, excited, and tingly all over when you first fell in love? Remember how high you felt, how right with the world? (Maybe you're lucky enough to be feeling that way right now!) Those physical sensations we call "falling in love" have a lot to do with phenylethylamine (pronounced "fen-el-eth-el-a-meen"), the chemical your brain secretes when you're deeply, romantically attracted to someone.

Chocolate contains phenylethylamine in the same form as the brain produces. Therefore, when you eat chocolate, you're apt to feel an enveloping sensation of warmth, tingles, and excitement similar to being in love.

Certain people—"chocoholics"—are especially attracted to these feelings, and this is the main reason they overeat chocolate. Studies conducted in 1987 by Margorie Schuman, Ph.D., a professor at the California School of Professional Psychology, bear this out. Schuman studied people who described themselves as having the following personality traits:

♥ Fall in love more easily than others

♥ Tend to be devastated by romantic rejection

♥ Are very sensitive to the approval or disapproval of others

♥ Like to be dramatic and/or flamboyant (this includes a need to be the center of attention)

♥ Experience frequent mood swings.

Dr. Schuman found that individuals with these characteristics often eat chocolate to "medicate" or cover up feelings of depression, tension, and irritability.

My 28-year-old client, Cathy, fit this profile perfectly. An executive secretary who attended college in the evening, Cathy felt extremely insecure when social conversations didn't revolve around her accomplishments. She was constantly telling her friends about the "A" she'd received on a test, or the report she'd finished for her boss. If the topic of discussion moved to another subject, Cathy would find some way to bring her friends' attention back to herself. Likewise, when she first came in for therapy, Cathy was reluctant to reveal anything less than flattering about herself to me, thinking that I'd reject her if I thought she were less than perfect.

Cathy's world also revolved around her constant, short-lived infatuations, usually with men completely wrong for her. During the first six months of our therapy, Cathy was sure that 10 different men were "Mr. Right." She'd talk briefly to a male student or to a new client at work, and, "Boom"—Cathy was swept off her feet.

For instance, there was 23-year-old Rick, who lived with his mother while he studied philosophy part time. Cathy was attracted to Rick's blazing green eyes and his lively classroom discussions about Soren Kierkegaard and Existentialism. One day after class, she walked with him out to the parking lot and asked for his phone number. That was the beginning, and for the next three weeks Cathy and Rick were inseparable—until the day Cathy called Rick and his mother answered the phone. When Rick's Mom innocently explained that Rick was "out with his girlfriend, Monica," Cathy promptly dropped out of Philosophy 101.

There were other men, all equally inappropriate and destructive to Cathy's self-esteem. Why would such a bright, attractive woman put herself in such demoralizing situations? What we discovered in therapy was that Cathy was addicted to her feelings of romantic love. The object of her affections—the man—wasn't that important. What did matter was that Cathy would constantly feel her favorite feeling of infatuation and everything that went with it: the butterflies in the stomach . . . the lighthearted feeling . . . the excited anticipation.

In the midst of all this, Cathy's self-image would swing from grandiosity to utter dejection. This is how she described her feelings, after she'd been in therapy for two months:

> Sometimes I feel like I'm the most powerful, beautiful, talented woman on earth. Like I could do anything—even own the whole world if I wanted to! I'd never admit those feelings to anyone else, because they'd think I was really stuck-up and wouldn't understand. But during those moments, I feel so high, so proud of who I am, and it's like nothing's gonna stop me from getting every one of my goals accomplished.
>
> Then something will happen, like my boss will find a mistake I did, or I'll break up with a boyfriend, and I suddenly feel like a world-class idiot. I'll get down on myself, saying things to myself like, "You jerk! How dare you think you could ever graduate from college or get a promotion at work! You're just a stupid idiot." Then I'll feel really depressed and I won't answer the phone or the doorbell 'cause I won't want to talk to anyone. And I won't want them to see me, because when I get that way, I feel so ugly.

During the times when Cathy felt, as she put it, "lower than a piece of dirt," she'd isolate herself from the outside world, close the curtains, and allow clutter and dirty dishes to pile up in her apartment. She would also binge on everything chocolate she could get her hands on: Haagen-Dazs chocolate ice cream, Oreo cookies, and even uncooked double-chocolate-chip cookie dough. Cathy would rationalize her eating by telling herself, "I deserve this," or, "Who cares how much I weigh? I don't ever want to be with a man again!"

Therapy, for Cathy, consisted of helping her to see how much power and control she was giving away to others. She was allowing others to decide how she felt about herself. If someone complimented Cathy, or if she received an "A," Cathy felt great about herself. If someone criticized her, or broke up with her, Cathy's self-esteem would plummet. When Cathy learned how to enjoy, but not to depend on, others' compliments and praise, she stopped having the wide swings in self-image.

Today, Cathy enjoys a successful relationship with a man who expresses a healthy, balanced level of appreciation toward Cathy. She says she feels unconditionally loved, and credits therapy for giving her insight into her previous destructive behavior that ended her other love relationships.

Chocolate and Your "Sexual Metabolism"

The ultimate aphrodisiac, I suppose, would be a chocolate-covered oyster. Of course, that doesn't sound very appetizing, but it does bring up the subject of sex—and its relationship to chocolate.

Unfortunately (and perhaps surprisingly), many chocoholics I've treated or interviewed reported dissatisfaction with their sex lives. As my client Cathy had done, they would console themselves for their feelings of loneliness and depression by eating chocolate. But by doing so, these chocoholics were also unwittingly adding to their sexual problems.

The majority of my sexually-dissatisfied clients were disinterested in having physical relationships with their spouses or their lovers. Most were also "autosexual," meaning that they preferred to receive sexual gratification through masturbation to intercourse.

As an example, let me share with you the story of my client Samantha, a pretty, 38-year-old supermarket cashier. Married for the second time four years before, Samantha told me she could hardly stand her husband to hold her or to kiss her. "It always starts out as a nice hug, but soon Rob wants me to take off my clothes and have sex with him," she complained. "It's easier just to stay away from him altogether, because I can't stand sex anymore."

Although Rob and Samantha had a romantic and sexually exciting first year of marriage, Samantha found herself losing interest in sex soon after they had their first child. The couple's sex life wasn't helped by the fact that during her pregnancy, Samantha had gained 50 pounds from eating a steady diet of chocolate ice cream and cheeseburgers, and was only able to lose 20 pounds after their daughter was born.

The weight gain had thrown Samantha for a loop— she'd never had a weight problem before! All of a sudden, Samantha felt matronly and ugly, and she didn't want Rob to look at her, let alone touch her. "It was like I had turned into my mother," Samantha remembered. "I saw myself as an old, fat woman with dimply cellulite on her thighs. And it's hard to be horny when you think you look like a cow. Rob always tells me my weight doesn't matter—he says there's more of me to love—but with this extra weight I just don't feel sexy anymore."

Samantha still eats chocolate every day, but she's switched from ice cream to frozen yogurt. Unfortunately, Samantha is choosing fattening versions of yogurt. A small or medium nonfat chocolate yogurt is one thing, but Samantha's favorite is a large low-fat chocolate yogurt with carob peanuts on top—a treat that adds almost 400 fat-laden calories to her daily diet.

Another client, 31-year-old Christine, seemingly had the opposite sexual problem from Samantha's. Christine had as insatiable an appetite for sex as she did for chocolate, and she could never get enough of either. She and her husband would have sex at least once a day during the week and several times during the weekend. And there's more: Christine also had a boyfriend with whom she slept two or three times a week.

Her preoccupation with sex was matched only by her obsession with chocolate. Christine was overweight in an extremely sexy, voluptuous, "Mae West" sort of way, and because her factory job surrounded her with men, she never lacked for sexual partners. During therapy, Christine complained that she felt controlled by her obsessions; she felt she had no choice but to have sex and to eat candy bars. Even though Christine felt unhappy in her marriage, she didn't want to leave her husband because "the sex is so great." And even though she desperately wanted to lose 40 pounds, she couldn't stay away from the candy vending machines because "chocolate tastes so great and makes me feel so good."

Both Samantha and Christine learned how their chocoholism was both a cause and an effect of their sexual problems. For Samantha and other women and men disinterested in sex or physical contact, the abuse of chocolate and other stimulant foods (colas, coffee, tea, and sugared foods) can lead to tremendous amounts of tension and irritability. Many people abuse the chief stimulants in chocolate—theobromine and tyramine—which instantly raise blood pressure and make you feel like you're raring to go. They crave energy, so they binge on chocolate.

While the amount of caffeine in chocolate is relatively small compared to, say, a cup of coffee, this stimulant still contributes to a feeling of being "up" after you've ingested it in chocolate. Add to this the blood sugar boost from the refined sugar, and it's easy to see why chocoholics use this food like a drug to get them going when they feel sluggish.

Unfortunately, after eating these pep foods all day long, it's difficult to unwind. Sexual enjoyment depends on being able to relax and to enjoy the sensations of your body, as well as that of your partner. If, however, you're uptight, tense, and irritable, you're more likely to get in an argument than into a romantic mood. As we discussed in previous chapters, sexual arousal depends on relaxation, so that the parasympathetic branch of the central nervous system can operate.

Eating stimulant foods for energy also creates a cycle of dependency. Let me explain. If you pump yourself up with chocolate, caffeine, and sugar all day long, you'll have to ingest a downer, or depressant, in the evening in order to slow down and to get some sleep.

Many people turn to alcohol or soothing foods such as breads or dairy products to fall asleep at night. They aren't able to have a full, restful night's sleep, however, because of the remaining effects of caffeine. They wake up feeling exhausted, and their serotonin level—the brain chemical that regulates mood, energy, and sexual arousal—is depleted. Then, because they're so sleepy in the morning, they reach for more caffeine, chocolate, or sugar to get going again. It's very easy to get into this pattern and not to know how to break out of it.

For hypersexual chocoholics like Christine, eating chocolate in abundance also plays a role in an imbalanced "sexual metabolism" (what I call the desire for sex, or the sexual appetite). Some people, as described above, clam up, isolate themselves, and feel tense after ingesting a lot of stimulant foods and beverages. Others like Christine, "act out," or become flamboyantly extroverted in response to pep foods. The stimulation Christine received from the chemicals in chocolate made her excited and anxious to receive sexual attention.

What we found in therapy, though, was illuminating: Christine's desire for sex and sexual advances was a lot like Cathy's obsession with compliments and praise. Christine, although she definitely enjoyed physical intercourse for its own merits, was mainly interested in being "validated" by it. She felt more worthwhile, more valuable as a woman, if she made a man want to go to bed with her. Obtaining a man's sexual interest was as much an accomplishment to Christine as an "A" on a test was to Cathy.

Chocolate For Two

While too much chocolate, like too much of any mood-altering chemical, can spoil romantic feelings, a little chocolate can go a long way! A moderate portion of chocolate can elevate mood and energy and put a couple in the mood for romance, passion, and fantastic lovemaking.

After a small to medium serving of one of the previous dinner suggestions, eat a small serving of a rich, decadent chocolate dessert. Serving size suggestions are listed with each recipe below. The idea is to have enough dessert to satisfy your appetite and your sweet tooth, as well as to create the feelings that lead to passion. If you eat too little, you won't feel any effects, and you may feel deprived. If you eat too much dessert, you'll feel overly full and sluggish. You'll want to nap instead of make love.

If you do feel too full after dinner and dessert, why not take a walk together to unwind and to digest your food? Walks are good ways for couples to focus on each other, without competing with the television, children, or telephones.

When eating dessert with your lover, make it a sensual experience. Keep the candles lit and the music soft. Feed each other bites of food, and you'll probably end up giggling and laughing. It's fun to put forks full of cheesecake into one each other's mouths. Try teasing your partner a bit. Let him eat only one tiny bite. Or ask her to close her eyes and to stick her tongue out. Then put the creamy dessert on her tongue and watch her enjoy the dessert's texture and taste.

One woman decided to slather chocolate mousse on her husband's penis, and they both enjoyed her licking it off immensely! You can try this with other recipes, or with ingredients like whipped cream or chocolate liqueur. And there's a lot of places like bellybuttons and nipples that are appropriate dessert-serving spots. Use your imagination—and have fun!

The Food-Mood Connection

As we discussed in the last chapter, combining carbohydrates and dairy products is an effective way to increase the brain's supply of serotonin. When serotonin levels are sufficient, our moods, energy levels, and sexual arousal potentials are stable. With adequate serotonin, we feel "good."

When you mix carbohydrates and dairy products with chocolate you get an especially potent combination. Desserts based on this mixture, especially desserts with a creamy texture, create quick jolts of euphoria. Take a look at a breakdown of some of the properties in the cheesecake recipes outlined in this chapter:

Ingredient/Characteristic Effect

♥ Choline   Soothing

♥ L-Tryptophane
with carbohydrates   Calming

♥ Creamy texture   Comforting

♥ Sugar   Temporarily energizing

♥ PEA   Feeling loved

♥ Theobromine   Temporarily energizing

♥ Tyramine   Temporarily energizing

♥ Caffeine   Temporarily energizing

♥ Magnesium   Relaxing

♥ Pyrazine   Pleasure inducing

And this is an incomplete list! This information should make it clear to you that cheesecakes with chocolate make you feel soothed and comforted while at the same time energizing you. In other words, after eating chocolate cheesecake, you feel renewed and ready to go. This is extremely similar to the way that prescription antidepressant drugs affect the mind and the body. Chocolate desserts that are based on dairy products are incredibly powerful antidepressant drugs, and they're over the counter!

Small portions of these desserts won't disrupt moderate diets, as long as your overall diet and exercise program keeps you active, with a low fat intake. I regularly eat small servings of dessert without gaining weight, just by watching my meal size and maintaining a regular exercise program. Keep in mind that lovemaking burns about 300 calories an hour!

The recipes in this chapter are divided into two sections: a decadent section and a light section. The decadent recipes use real butter, cream, and chocolate. The studies about trans-fatty acids in margarine, which can raise serum cholesterol levels, have changed the way I cook. Margarine and other synthetic foods have potentially health-damaging properties. I would rather eat small portions of natural foods than large portions of artificial foods. I also believe that the tastes, smells, and textures of foods cooked with butter are superior to those cooked with margarine.

In the "light" section of this chapter, I have included recipes for low-fat, low-sugar versions of the desserts. Frankly, they don't taste or look as wonderful as the decadent desserts, but they do contain the mood-altering chemicals that can lead to euphoric passion. And they're much lower in calories and fat, so you may enjoy a larger portion without feeling guilty.

A 1978 study conducted by David Kritchevsky, Ph.D., at the University of Pennsylvania, yielded some interesting results on the effects of the fat in chocolate on serum cholesterol. The study supported other research that showed that the stearic acid in chocolate may offset, or cancel out, the saturated fat in cocoa butter. In other words, the fat in chocolate behaves differently from the fat from other sources. The stearic acid in chocolate "rescues" the serum cholesterol before the cocoa butter has a chance to raise it.

Decadent Desserts For Lovers

Chocolate Climax Cheesecake

This chocolate cheesecake is layered between an extra-rich chocolate graham cookie crust and a chocolate mousse topping. The results will make you feel proud of your accomplishment, and heightened with anticipation.

Chocolate Cheesecake Crust

1 1/2 cups crushed chocolate graham crackers
3 Tablespoons white granulated sugar
1/2 cup (1 stick) butter
3 squares semi-sweet baking chocolate

Preheat oven to 325 degrees (F).

In a deep bowl, thoroughly mix graham crackers and sugar. Over low heat or in double-boiler, slowly melt butter and baking chocolate, stirring constantly. Pour melted mixture into graham crackers and mix with large spoon until thoroughly blended.

Press mixture into greased and floured 9-inch springboard baking pan, bringing the crust up the pan sides approximately 1 1/2 inches. Make certain crust is evenly distributed on bottom and sides. Bake at 325 degrees for 10 minutes. Once crust is cooked, cool in the refrigerator and reduce oven heat to 300 degrees.

Chocolate Cheesecake Filling

2 eight-ounce packages cream cheese, softened to room
    temperature
1/2 cup white granulated sugar
1/2 teaspoon vanilla extract
12 semi-sweet baking chocolate squares

2 eggs, separated with egg whites in deep bowl (prefer-
ably copper, if you have one)

In deep bowl, blend cream cheese, sugar. and vanilla
with large spoon. Slowly melt chocolate over low heat or
double-boiler, stirring constantly. Add melted chocolate
to cream cheese mixture and blend with a hand mixer at
low-speed for 1 minute, adding egg yolks. Thoroughly
wash and dry mixer beaters and, in a separate bowl, beat
egg whites until stiff. Fold egg whites into cheesecake
mixture and blend 1 minute at low speed, scraping sides
of bowl. Pour mixture into pan and crust.

Put very hot tap water into shallow, oven-proof pan or
bowl, and place this on the bottom rack of the oven. This
will help to keep the cheesecake moist as it bakes. Put
cheesecake in oven, taking care to center it so heat is
distributed evenly. Bake 45 minutes at 300 degrees.

Chocolate Mousse Topping
1 cup milk chocolate chips
1/2 cup (1 stick) butter
4 teaspoons white granulated sugar
4 eggs, separated with egg whites in deep bowl (prefer-
ably copper, if you have one)

In deep pot, melt chocolate chips and butter over low
heat, stirring constantly. Reduce heat to its minimum
setting, and stir in sugar. Remove pot from heat and
quickly add egg yolks one at a time, mixing with large
fork as each yolk is added.

Using hand mixer at medium speed, whip egg whites
until stiff, fold into chocolate mixture, and stir with fork.
Place in refrigerator until cheesecake is baked. Pour over
baked cheesecake and place in refrigerator approximately
5-6 hours (best if left overnight before serving).

Adam-and-Eve Fudge Brownie Cheesecake

This superb, classic cheesecake sits between a fudge layer and a topping of chocolate "Adam and Eve" fig leaves and berries. An erotic experience for the eyes and the taste buds, you'll love the reactions this dessert evokes!

Fudge Bottom
1/2 cup (1 stick) butter
4 one-ounce squares unsweetened baking chocolate
1 1/2 cups granulated white sugar
2 medium or large eggs
1/4 cup milk
1 teaspoon vanilla extract
1 cup all-purpose flour
1/2 teaspoon salt

Cheesecake Filling
3 eight-ounce packages cream cheese, softened to room
    temperature
3/4 cup granulated white sugar
1 teaspoon vanilla extract
3 medium or large eggs
1/2 cup sour cream

Cheesecake Topping
1 cup sour cream
2 Tablespoons granulated white sugar
1 teaspoon vanilla extract

Adam and Eve Fig Leaves
4 one-ounce squares sweet baking chocolate

10 - 15 thoroughly washed and dried leaves from fruit-
bearing plant (such as grape, apple, pear, fig, or peach
tree) or from a rose bush
10 washed and dried berries (any type) or cherries

Fudge bottom preparation

Preheat oven to 325 degrees (F). Lightly grease and flour
a 9- or 9 1/2 inch springform pan.

Slowly melt butter and chocolate together over very
low heat in heavy saucepan or double-boiler, stirring
constantly. An alternative method of melting butter and
chocolate is to heat them in microwave oven in a glass
bowl for 1 minute at high heat, then stir together and cook
them for an additional 30 seconds.

Stir in sugar until thoroughly blended. Add one egg at
a time, blending into mixture. Add milk and vanilla, and
after they are thoroughly mixed, stir in flour and salt. Mix
entire ingredients by hand with large spoon until mixture
is a consistent smooth, dark-brown blend.

Spoon the fudge mixture evenly across bottom of
springform pan (mixture will not go up sides as in a
traditional graham cracker cheesecake crust).

Cheesecake filling preparation

Using mixer at medium speed, blend together cream
cheese, sugar, and vanilla extract. Add eggs one at a time,
blending well after each addition. Blend in sour cream an
additional minute. Do not overbeat.

Pour cheesecake filling over fudge bottom. The springform pan will be almost completely filled, but cheesecake
levels lower slightly during the cooking process. Place
cheesecake in center of preheated oven. On rack below
cheesecake, put pan of hot water (the humidity will help
cheesecake retain its moisture). Bake 50 minutes, or until
center is almost set.

Cheesecake topping preparation

When the cheesecake bottom and filling have 10-15 minutes cooking time remaining, prepare the cheesecake topping. Mix sour cream, sugar, and vanilla extract with large spoon. Spread evenly over cheesecake when baking time is completed.

Return cheesecake to oven, still at 325 degrees, for an additional 10 minutes. After baking, run a long knife along edges of cheesecake to loosen gently. Immediately put cheesecake in refrigerator, and let sit at least 4 hours before serving.

Adam and Eve fig leaves decoration preparation

(*Note:* Don't let this topping intimidate you, because you'll find chocolate leaves to be a simple, yet impressive, way to top this perfect cheesecake!)

Melt chocolate squares either slowly over low heat, stirring frequently, *or* in microwave oven on high power for 1 minute, then stirring and heating additional 30 seconds at high heat.

While chocolate cools slightly, spread waxed paper over a large plate or cookie sheet. Using narrow spatula or knife, "paint" the chocolate over the undersides of each leaf. Don't worry about perfectly covering each leaf with chocolate, but do avoid allowing the chocolate to run under the edges of the leaf. Place "painted" leaves on waxed paper surface and refrigerate approximately 1/2 hour, or until chocolate is firm.

When cheesecake is cooled, arrange chocolate leaves (once cooled, the leaves will peel easily from the chocolate) with berries in clusters around cheesecake edges, or in one large bouquet in center.

Pecan-Chocolate Fantasy Cheesecake

This is one of the richest cheesecakes I've ever tasted. It is absolutely delicious and very gooey, so a little goes a long way!

Chocolate Crust

1 package (10 ounces) chocolate wafer cookies, crushed
    into crumbs
1/4 cup (1/2 stick) butter, melted
2 Tablespoons granulated white sugar

Combine cookie crumbs, butter and sugar in bowl. Spoon into 9 or 9 1/2" springform pan and press evenly onto bottom and one inch up sides of pan. Set aside.

Milk Chocolate Mousse Syrup

3 cups milk chocolate pieces or chips
3 Tablespoons sugar
1 cup heavy whipping cream
1 1/2 teaspoons vanilla extract
4 Tablespoons butter
2 egg yolks, beaten

Preheat oven to 325 degrees (F).

Melt chocolate pieces over low heat on stove top or at high setting in microwave oven for 1 minute, then stirring and heating additional 30 seconds at high heat. Stir in sugar, whipping cream, and vanilla extract. Return mixture to heat for 2 minutes. Stir until mixture is thick and smooth. Stir in butter until it melts and is blended into mixture. Mix in egg yolks and stir well, about 1 minute. Place mixture in refrigerator while you prepare the cheesecake filling.

Cheesecake Filling
3 eight-ounce packages cream cheese, softened
1 cup sugar
3 eggs
1 Tablespoon vanilla extract
1/2 cup whipping cream
2 cups chopped pecans

In large bowl, combine cream cheese and sugar and blend at medium speed until smooth. Add eggs one at time, keeping mixer at low speed. Blend in vanilla and whipping cream and turn mixer to medium speed for three minutes, scraping sides of bowl.

Pour 1/2 cheesecake filling over chocolate crust in springform pan. Pour 1/2 chocolate mousse syrup over cheesecake filling, and then pour remaining half of cheesecake over syrup. Sprinkle pecans over top of cake.

Bake for 75 minutes, or until cheesecake is almost set in the center. Place cheesecake in refrigerator immediately. One hour later, pour remaining chocolate syrup over top of cheesecake. Refrigerate at least 5 hours or overnight before serving.

Cook's Note: This is a delicious cake, but one with a very gooey texture. The cheesecake must be thoroughly cooled before being removed from the springform pan, or it will fall.

Double Fudge Chocolate Chip Cookies

This twist on an old favorite will take the two of you back to your fondest childhood memories of cookies and milk after school.

3/4 cup light brown sugar, firmly packed
1/2 cup granulated white sugar
1 cup (2 sticks) softened butter
1 teaspoon vanilla
1 medium egg
1 3/4 cups all-purpose baking flour
1/4 cup unsweetened cocoa powder
1 teaspoon baking soda
1/2 teaspoon salt
1 package (11.5 ounces) milk chocolate chips (not semi-sweet)
1 cup chopped pecans
2 high-quality cookie sheets

Preheat oven to 375 degrees (F).

In large bowl, blend brown sugar, granulated sugar and butter on medium speed for 2 minutes. Add vanilla and egg, and blend an additional 2 minutes at medium speed. In separate bowl, mix flour, cocoa, baking soda, and salt together thoroughly. Add flour mixture to sugar mixture and blend at medium speed until light and fluffy.

Using large spoon, gently stir in chocolate chips and pecans. Drop dough by rounded teaspoonfuls onto ungreased cookie sheets. Bake in center of oven at 375 degrees for 9-12 minutes or until firm in center. Don't burn the undersides! While one sheet is baking, prepare the other for baking—makes it go faster and smoother! You'll be making a couple of batches per sheet. The sheets do not need to be cool. Makes 3-4 dozen cookies.

Chocolate Truffle Balls

This is a deceptively simple recipe that will yield delicious balls you can pop into each other's mouths!

1/2 cup heavy whipping cream
3 Tablespoons butter
2 Tablespoons granulated white sugar
2 four-ounce packages sweet baking chocolate
Optional: 1 Tablespoon liqueur, such as coffee, chocolate, or orange liqueur
For coating, you may use one or more of the following: ground walnuts, pecans, or almonds, cocoa powder, shredded coconut, chocolate sprinkles, rainbow sprinkles, crushed cookies, or powdered sugar.

Put whipping cream, butter, and sugar in medium bowl and heat in microwave oven on high heat for 1 1/2 minutes. Stir the ingredients and heat an additional 1 1/2 minutes, so that mixture comes to a boil.

Add chocolate and stir until chocolate is melted and thoroughly blended with mixture. Add liqueur, if desired.

Cook's Note: If liqueur is not added, substitute 1 teaspoon vanilla extract.

Refrigerate approximately 2 hours, or until mixture is firm.

Form chocolate mixture into 1-inch balls. Roll each ball in one of desired coatings and return balls to refrigerator until ready to serve. Truffles can be served in candy paper cups, or with decorative toothpicks.

Sweetheart Cookies

These heart-shaped chocolate cookies drizzled with a chocolate glaze are delightful finger-foods. Try them with chocolate ice cream, or for a treat that will make you feel like a kid again, try dipping them in milk.

3 sticks butter, softened
1 1/4 cup granulated white sugar
1 Tablespoon vanilla extract
2 3/4 cups all-purpose flour
1/4 cup unsweetened cocoa powder
1 1/2 cups sweetened milk chocolate chips

Blend butter and sugar with electric hand mixer on medium speed. When mixture is thoroughly blended, mix in vanilla extract. Slowly add flour and cocoa powder, blending thoroughly at low speed. Cover mixture and place in refrigerator for 1 hour.

Heat oven to 325 degrees (F). Take cookie dough out of refrigerator and place on floured board. Flatten mixture by hand and then roll with floured rolling pin to 1/4" thickness. Cut into heart shapes with cookie cutter and bake on ungreased cookie sheet for 15-17 minutes. Transfer cookies to wax-paper-covered plate after baking.

Meanwhile, melt chocolate chips in microwave oven at 50-percent power for 1 minute. Stir and return to microwave for additional 30 seconds at same power.

Using small spoon, drizzle melted chocolate over cookies in free-form lacy pattern. Place cookies in refrigerator to harden chocolate glaze.

Peanut Butter Cup Cookies

These chocolate and peanut butter cookies will remind you of your favorite peanut butter cup candies. You'll be in the mood to play after you eat a few of these!

Chocolate Cookie

3 ounces unsweetened baking chocolate
2 sticks butter, softened
1 cup white granulated sugar
1 medium egg
1 teaspoon vanilla extract
2 cups all-purpose flour
1 teaspoon baking soda
1/8 teaspoon salt

Melt chocolate and butter over low heat in medium pan, stirring constantly to avoid burning, until chocolate is completely melted and blended into butter. Stir sugar into mixture and slowly add egg and vanilla extract, until all are thoroughly blended. Pour mixture into large mixing bowl. Blend in flour, baking soda and salt. Cover with plastic wrap and refrigerate 30 minutes while preparing peanut butter cup filling.

Peanut Butter Cup Filling

3/4 cup smooth peanut butter
1/2 stick butter, softened
2 Tablespoons heavy whipping cream
1 teaspoon vanilla extract
1 1/2 cups white granulated sugar

Blend peanut butter and butter on medium speed for one minute. Slowly pour in cream and vanilla extract and continue beating an additional minute. Add sugar and mix thoroughly 2 minutes, scraping sides of bowl with hand mixer. Cover and refrigerate.

Remove cookie dough from refrigerator and shape into 1-inch balls for cookies. Flatten balls into round, flat shapes on ungreased cookie sheet and bake 8-10 minutes at 350 degrees. Remove from cookie sheet and flatten with spatula. Cool cookies in refrigerator.

When cookies are completely cooled, spread peanut butter filling generously between two cookies. Press cookies together, like a sandwich. Dip 1/2 each cookie sandwich in chocolate candy coating and place on wax paper in refrigerator for 1 hour before serving.

Chocolate Candy Coating
1 cup milk chocolate chips

Melt chocolate chips over low heat, stirring constantly to avoid burning, or on high power in micowave oven for 1 minute, then stirring and heating additional 30 seconds at high heat. Dip 1/2 sandwich cookies in chocolate mixture.

Chocolate Seduction Cake

This is a beautifully romantic cake to serve by candlelight. It's the ultimate in rich, moist chocolate cake with a decadent fudge frosting that is guaranteed to impress. Because it is so rich and delicious, you'll savor each bite as it melts in your mouth. Enjoy!

Cake

4 ounces unsweetened baking chocolate
1 3/4 cups granulated white sugar
1 1/4 cups milk
1 stick butter, softened
3 medium eggs
1 2/3 cups all-purpose flour
1 teaspoon baking soda
1/8 teaspoon salt
1 teaspoon vanilla extract

Preheat oven to 350 degrees (F).

Heat chocolate, 1/2 cup milk, and 1/2 cup sugar over low heat, stirring constantly until chocolate is melted and mixture thoroughly blended. Set aside to allow mixture to cool.

In large bowl, beat butter and remaining sugar on low speed for 2 minutes. Add eggs, one at a time, keeping mixer at low speed as each egg is blended. Add the remaining milk and blend 1 minute. Slowly add flour, baking soda, and salt, and mix until smooth. Blend in chocolate mixture and vanilla extract. Pour cake batter into two 9-inch layer pans, lightly greased and floured.

Bake in 350 degree oven 30-35 minutes or until cake is set in center. Frost with chocolate seduction frosting between two layers and on top of cake. Garnish with raspberries or crushed walnuts.

Chocolate Seduction Frosting
4 squares unsweetened baking chocolate
2 Tablespoons butter, softened
4 cups powdered sugar
1/2 cup milk
1 teaspoon vanilla extract

Melt chocolate and butter on low heat, stirring until both are melted and blended. Or put on high power in microwave for 1 minute, then stirring and heating additional 30 seconds at high heat. Stir in sugar, milk, and vanilla extract until mixture is thick and smooth.

Sex Appeal Apple Pie

The sex appeal of this delicious pie is three-fold: First, it will bring back fond memories of eating apple pie as a child, and it will put you in a fun-filled, childlike mood; second, apple pie is a classic "comfort" food, which feels and tastes good to eat; third, the delicious ingredients are high in carbohydrates. If you eat the pie *à la mode* with vanilla ice cream, you'll be combining tryptophan and carbohydrates for a high serotonin-producing treat.

Double-Crust
3 cups all-purpose flour
1 teaspoon salt
2 teaspoons white granulated sugar
1 cup butter (2 sticks)
6 - 8 Tablespoons ice water

Mix flour, salt, and sugar together in large mixing bowl. With pastry cutter or 2 knives, cut in butter with flour until dough becomes a coarse, mealy texture.

Add ice water and blend until dough can be gathered into a ball. Divide ball into 2 halves, cover, and refrigerate both halves for a 1/2 hour. Roll out each crust using floured rolling pin and floured surface. Flour your hands to prevent sticking, and work crust into an even, flat surface. Measure crust as you go by occasionally placing the top side of a 9-inch pie pan down on the crust. The crust should measure 1 inch larger around than edges of the pie pan.

You are making 2 crusts, one for the bottom and one for the top. Fold crust for pie bottom in half, then in half again. Place folded crust on bottom of the pie pan and unfold so crust is evenly centered. Place top crust aside until pie is filled with nut and apple mixtures.

Nut Mixture Filling

1 cup crushed walnuts
3 Tablespoons packed brown sugar
2 Tablespoons beaten egg (yolk and white)
1 Tablespoon milk
1 Tablespoon butter, softened
1/4 teaspoon vanilla extract
1/8 teaspoon ground cinnamon
1/4 teaspoon lemon juice

Combine nuts, brown sugar, egg, and milk until thoroughly blended. Add butter, vanilla, cinnamon, and lemon juice. Spread mixture evenly over bottom of unbaked pie crust.

Apple Filling

5 cups peeled and sliced apples (about 2 pounds or 6
    medium Golden Delicious apples)
1 teaspoon lemon juice
1 cup granulated sugar
2 Tablespoons all-purpose flour
1 teaspoon ground cinnamon
1 teaspoon ground nutmeg
1/4 teaspoon salt
2 Tablespoons butter

Place apple slices in large bowl and sprinkle with lemon juice. In separate bowl combine sugar, flour, cinnamon, nutmeg, and salt. Pour mixture over apples and stir well. Spoon apple filling over nut mixture. Place small dots of butter evenly over apples. Moisten crust edges with water.

Place top crust carefully over pie, pressing edges together with a large fork, and remoistening as needed. Cut slits into top crust to allow steam to escape during baking. Beat 1 egg together with 1 1/2 Tablespoons granulated sugar and brush mixture evenly over crust. The egg and sugar will make a beautiful, sweet glaze for the crust.

Bake in center of oven at 425 degrees for 50 minutes, or until filling in center is bubbly and crust is golden brown. You can avoid burning the pie crust edges by covering them with long strings of aluminum foil.

Chocolate-Dipped Strawberries and Champagne (or Ginger Ale)

This is a classic light dessert that sets the tone for romance and decadence. To add a sexy touch, take turns feeding each other the strawberries.

4 one-ounce squares sweetened baking chocolate
12-20 firm, ripe, fresh strawberries with stems, thoroughly
washed and dried

Melt chocolate either slowly over very low heat, stirring constantly, *or* in microwave oven on high heat for 1 minute, stirring well and returning for additional 30 seconds at high heat.

Hold strawberries by stems and dip bottom half into chocolate. Place dipped strawberries on wax paper and refrigerate until firm, at least 1/2 hour.

Cook's note: If chocolate cools too much to coat strawberries smoothly, reheat chocolate slightly.

Presentation suggestion: Place wet champagne flutes in freezer for 1 hour, to "frost" them before serving champagne or ginger ale.

Float strawberry (without chocolate) in each glass.

Light and Delicious Chocolate Desserts

These desserts are lower in fat than the previous recipes. They are as delicious as low-fat desserts can be. Unfortunately, nothing tastes as good as desserts made with real butter, eggs, and sugar. But for those of us watching our fat, calorie, or cholesterol intake, forsaking a little taste for health can be well worth it.

The ingredients in these desserts include fructose, the fruit sugar sweetener available in health food stores and some supermarkets. There is evidence that fructose is easier to digest than granulated white sugar, and fructose may keep your blood sugar level more stable after ingestion than more refined sugars typically do.

The dessert recipes also call for whole wheat flour, egg substitute (found in the freezer section of grocery stores), and low-calorie margarine. Please note that some very-low-calorie margarines are not appropriate for baking. They don't readily melt or blend with other ingredients. For this reason, I prefer *slightly*-reduced calorie margarine to light varieties.

Delicious Home-Style Chocolate Chip Cookies

Makes 15 cookies (97 calories and 3 grams of fat each).

Low-calorie chocolate chips

1/2 ounce (1 square) unsweetened baking chocolate
1 Tablespoon low-calorie margarine
2 Tablespoons granulated fructose sugar
1/16 teaspoon (approximately 2 pinches) cream of tartar

Preheat oven to 375 degrees (F) and spray nonstick cooking spray on a cookie sheet.

In a microwave-proof bowl, cook chocolate and margarine together in microwave oven for 1 1/2 minutes on high.

Stir together to complete melting process for chocolate. Add fructose and cream of tartar, and mix thoroughly.

Allow mixture to cool 2 minutes and then spoon mixture onto large sheet of waxed paper, making tiny "chip-size" drops about 1/3" in diameter. Put waxed paper and chips in freezer. Allow chips to freeze until completely solid, about 30-45 minutes. Chips can then be used like regular chocolate chips, and will fold into cookie batter easily.

Cookie Batter

1/3 cup low-calorie margarine, softened
3/4 cup granulated fructose sugar
1/4 cup egg substitute
1/2 teaspoon vanilla extract
3/4 cup whole wheat flour
1/4 teaspoon baking powder

In bowl, blend margarine, fructose, egg substitute and vanilla together thoroughly. Add flour and baking powder, and stir until batter is completely mixed. Carefully fold in Chocolate Chips and spoon onto cookie sheet to make 15 cookies. Bake 7-9 minutes.

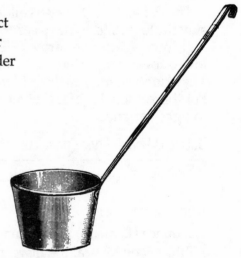

Moist and Chewy Brownies

Makes 16 brownies, 52 calories and 2 grams of fat each.

1/2 ounce (1 square) unsweetened baking chocolate
1/4 cup low-calorie margarine
1/8 teaspoon cream of tartar
1/4 cup egg substitute
1/2 cup granulated fructose sugar
1 teaspoon vanilla extract
1/4 cup whole wheat flour

Preheat oven to 350 degrees and spray nonstick cooking spray on the bottom and sides of 8" x 8" baking pan.

Melt chocolate and margarine together in large microwave-proof bowl in microwave oven for 1 1/2 minutes on high. Stir until chocolate is completely melted and mixed with margarine.

Stir in remaining ingredients, one by one, until batter is completely blended. Pour batter into cooking pan and bake 20-22 minutes. Brownies are done when center springs to the touch, or when a fork pierced through the middle is clean when removed. Cool completely, then cut into 16 brownies, 2" x 2" each.

Double-Chocolate Frosted Cake

Makes 16 pieces, each approximately 2" x 2", 72 calories, and 1.6 grams fat.

Cake
1/2 ounce (1 square) unsweetened baking chocolate
1 teaspoon low-calorie margarine
1/4 teaspoon vanilla extract
1/8 teaspoon cream of tartar
1/2 cup granulated fructose sugar
3/4 cup nonfat milk
1 Tablespoon honey
2 Tablespoons unsweetened cocoa powder
2/3 cup whole wheat flour
1 teaspoon baking powder
1/4 cup egg substitute

Preheat oven to 350 degrees (F). Spray nonstick cooking spray on bottom and sides of 8" x 8" baking pan.

Place baking chocolate, margarine, vanilla extract, and cream of tartar into large microwave-proof bowl, and cook in microwave oven on high for 1 1/2 minutes. Stir until chocolate is completely melted and ingredients blended.

Stir in remaining ingredients, one at a time, until batter is completely blended. Pour batter into baking pan and bake 20 minutes. After baking, allow cake to cool in baking pan 30 minutes before frosting with Chocolate Frosting.

Frosting
2 Tablespoons low-calorie margarine, softened
1 Tablespoon unsweetened cocoa powder

3 Tablespoons granulated fructose sugar

Using back of large spoon, blend ingredients until mixture is smooth and uniform in color. Spread frosting on top of cooled cake.

Non-Fat Devil's Food Cookies

Makes 12 cookies, 75 calories, and less than 1 gram of fat each.

Ingredients and Preparation

2 Tablespoons unsweetened cocoa powder
1/2 cup light corn syrup
2 Tablespoons (1/8 cup) egg substitute
3 Tablespoons nonfat milk
1/4 teaspoon baking powder
1 Tablespoon honey
3/4 cup whole wheat flour

Preheat oven to 325 degrees (F) and spray nonstick cooking spray on cookie sheet.

Blend cocoa powder, corn syrup, egg substitute, and milk together in large bowl. Stir in baking powder and honey. Add flour and blend completely.

Spoon dough onto cookie sheet to make 12 cookies. Bake 5-7 minutes.

Low-Fat Chocolate Dream Mousse

Serves 2. 132 calories and 2 grams of fat per serving.

2 1/2 cups water
2 envelopes (1/4 ounce each) plain gelatin powder
6 Tablespoons evaporated skim milk
14 packets Equal or Nutrasweet (not saccharine) sweetener
1/2 cup powdered nonfat milk
2 Tablespoons unsweetened cocoa powder

Bring 1 1/2 cups water to rolling boil (you are boiling more water than you need because part of the water will evaporate). Pour 1 cup boiling water into deep bowl and mix hot water and gelatin with electric mixer on medium speed for 1 minute. Add 1 cup cold water and beat additional minute. Add evaporated milk and beat on medium speed until mixture is frothy. Cover and refrigerate 45 minutes.

Remove from refrigerator and add sweetener, nonfat milk powder, and cocoa powder. Beat on medium speed 2 minutes, until entire mixture attains thick, smooth consistency.

Chapter Twelve
Making The Earth Move

*"I love it when she's gentle with me and caresses me with a
lot of love and affection. My weakest parts are my earlobes.
When she kisses, pets, and licks my earlobes, I'm instantly
put in a romantic mood."—52-year-old married man*

You've just finished a delicious dinner and the two of you
are enjoying dessert while snuggling together on the
couch. Now what? Clearly, this moment represents a fork
in the road of passion. Your choices include turning on
the television until 11:30, then going to bed and gauging

whether you have any energy left for lovemaking—which you probably won't.

So many of us in long-term, committed relationships act like we're sleepwalking in the passion department. We go on automatic pilot, and our love partner becomes like a piece of furniture that's always there. We appreciate the other person, but we don't really notice him or her so much anymore.

To reignite passion, you'll need to retune your senses and *really* notice your love partner. You'll need to create a "love event" by doing something out of the ordinary. Here are a few prescriptions—*Do's* and *Don'ts*—for your after-dessert time:

♥ Don't turn on the television. It takes the focus off each other, numbs your senses, and pushes your body into a hibernation-like state. Your mental and physical energy levels drop.

♥ Do have a refreshing drink. This may include a small amount of alcohol or caffeine. Mineral water with a twist is very invigorating.

♥ Don't overdrink any liquid. Too much alcohol leads to sleepiness or irritability, and you'll either fall asleep or have an argument. Too much caffeine in colas, tea, or coffee can make you edgy.

♥ Do drink your liquids in a crystal goblet or another special-type glass. Serve your meal and dessert on special dishes, as well.

♥ Do light candles during dinner, and keep them lit until bed-time.

♥ Do have soft background music playing. Tapes or CDs are preferable to radio, since commercials and news breaks can interrupt a romantic interlude.

♥ Do wear a flattering outfit. Even though you've been with your romantic partner for some time, this is a special occasion well worth the effort of looking your best. You show respect for your partner when you dress nicely. This doesn't mean an evening gown or a tuxedo, but it does mean an outfit your partner doesn't normally see. Choose an outfit that makes you feel sexy.

♥ Don't answer the telephone or the door. Let the answering machine take calls for you, and don't check your messages until morning. Remember, even though you're at home, you are unavailable for the evening.

♥ Do have a child-free evening. This means arranging child-care away from the home, or at least a firm early bedtime. No exceptions.

♥ Don't clean the dishes, unless it's a mutual project. The idea is to be together, and if kitchen chores don't include the both of you, forget them until morning. If you wash and dry together, however, you can turn it into a quick, playful time. Try kissing her on the back of the neck as she washes the dishes. Try grabbing him from behind as he dries. Rub against each other. Flirt. Pinch. Pat. Bite. Stroke. And give plenty of kisses.

Flirting and Foreplay

You've undoubtedly read that telling your partner what you want sexually is best for you and your relationship. Yet many people resist discussing their sexual preferences openly. Perhaps it's an unspoken policy within the relationship not to talk about sex. Maybe one or both partners is shy about "dirty talk." Often, a person may not know exactly what he or she wants. More commonly, they don't know how to articulate their desires; they don't know how to put their sexual wants into words.

Everyone has different preferences about foreplay, yet there are common denominators that hold true for most men and women. After all, the physiology of men and women ensures that orgasm occurs in pretty universal ways. In other words, what turns on one man is likely to arouse another man. And the same applies to women.

Individual differences in sexual preferences occur because of experiences. Brian, for example, had learned how to masturbate by rubbing his penis up and down between his legs. Normal masturbation attempts, involving gripping the penis with a hand, didn't arouse him at all. The only way, outside of intercourse, that Brian could ejaculate was to push his erect penis up and down between his legs.

Carl also had developed a unique sexual preference. He had very sensitive testicles and found orgasms to be exceptionally pleasurable when his testicles were stimulated. When Carl masturbated, he would rub his testicles with the heel of one foot. And Carl's wife, Brenda, would cup them lightly in her hands during intercourse and when she masturbated him. Since Carl was very sensitive, Brenda was careful to touch his testicles very lightly. Any extra pressure created painful sensations that turned Carl off.

Mark, however, enjoyed a very firm touch. He liked his testicles and penis to be squeezed with a firm grip. He asked his fiancée to hold his testicles firmly at his moment of orgasm. She was concerned about hurting him, but Mark assured her that the firmer she squeezed, the more pleasure he received.

Women have similar differences in their sexual tastes. The only way Elizabeth could have an orgasm was through firm manual stimulation of her clitoris. Her husband learned the best way to bring Elizabeth to a climax by watching her masturbate. He then recreated her motions with his own hand.

Denise was accustomed to using a vibrator to stimulate an orgasm. Although she would love to orgasm with her hand or during sexual intercourse, Denise has been unsuccessful. "So I taught my husband how to make me come with my vibrator," Denise explained. "I was afraid he'd be jealous of my vibrator, but he loves using it on me. I love it too!"

Most women, like Denise, have difficulty orgasming during intercourse. Some studies indicate that 70 percent, or more, of women never orgasm during "normal" sexual intercourse.

Faking Orgasms— The Trap of Deceit

The unfortunate outgrowth of women's difficulties in having an orgasm during intercourse is that they often fake it. Women know how much men love it when they scream, sigh, and generally carry on about how great the sex is. In a new relationship where the woman feels insecure or uptight, she may fake an orgasm just to please him. In a long-term relationship, she may pretend to come, just to hurry up the intercourse and get it over with.

Problems begin the minute she fakes an orgasm. She's then trapped in the deceit. Judy's story is very typical of the mess that occurs when women pretend to "come":

> When John and I were just starting out, he had just broken up with a woman named Marie. Marie and John had been engaged to be married, and he had been crazily in love with her. Then Marie went and married another guy. John was heartbroken when I met him,

and I helped him get his head back together. But in the beginning, all I ever heard about was how wonderful Marie was.

Apparently, Marie had been pretty hot in bed. Frankly, she sounds like a real bitch to me and I think sex was the real reason John was so crazy about her. Anyway, by the time John and I became an item and started sleeping together, I felt like I was competing with Marie, in a way. I wanted to be better in bed than she was. So I pretended to have these massive, hot orgasms. I'd scream and rock my body all over the place.

Judy was quiet for a long moment before continuing. She pushed her long black hair away from her eyes and sighed deeply, as though out of regret. She absent-mindedly played with the large wedding ring on her finger. "John would hold me tight and ask me if I'd come good. I always went on and on about what a great lover he was." Eventually, John stopped talking about Marie. Judy and John were married three months after they'd met.

"We have a really good marriage," sighed Judy. "It's just that I don't know what to do about the sex." Judy explained that she never had an orgasm during intercourse, because she couldn't explain her sexual preferences to John. "He already thinks he's getting me off real good. How can I ask him to change the way he makes love to me?"

Judy feels trapped. She's tried stopping her faked orgasms. "But then John acts depressed that he didn't make me come. Or, he'll keep making love a *long* time to try to give me an orgasm. So I'm forced to keep up my act, so *he'll* at least enjoy himself."

Judy's sexual outlet involves masturbating when John's at work. Lately, she's been fantasizing about having an affair. "I love John very much," Judy cautiously explained. "But sometimes I think how nice it would be to start over with a new guy, and to show him from the start how to use his hands and tongue to make me really have an orgasm. I can't admit the truth to John. He'd be devastated and really pissed off at me for lying to him. I just feel so trapped!"

For women like Judy, who feel caught in a web of faked orgasms, there is a solution. You'll need to tell your man you've read about a new way to have a super-charged orgasm. Believe me, this will peak any man's interest. Then it's up to you to decide how to convey your sexual preferences to your man.

You can masturbate in front of him. Men really love this. Just watch any soft- or hard-porn video and you'll see how much film time is devoted to women making themselves orgasm. If you need to have a small glass of wine to relax, then do so. Or try having a really great fantasy in mind. For instance, imagine you're a sex film star and your partner is the film director.

Then help him recreate your masturbation actions with his own hand. Show him how firm you like the touch, and how fast you prefer the hand action. If you're using a vibrator, show him the best way to hold it. He'll appreciate the guidance and you'll appreciate the results.

If you don't want to masturbate in front of him, you can hand him sexy literature (such as this book) that lists step-by-step instructions. You can explore together the adventure of sharing orgasms.

Once he's mastered the art of bringing you to orgasm, you can gradually stop faking orgasms during sex. Tell him that the (real) orgasms he's been giving you are so satisfying that you prefer those. All he really wants is for you to be sexually satisfied and to view him as your sexual hero. So compliment him and encourage him to keep up the good work. You'll both win as a result.

Oral Sex For Him

The first time I heard the term "blow job," I was confused. I asked a sexually-experienced friend of mine what it meant. Was I supposed to blow air on the penis? What was I supposed to do? My friend was equally oblivious.

It wasn't until my college courses on human sexuality that I really learned the intricate details about pleasuring a man with oral sex. Again, everyone is different and has varying tastes and preferences. But here is the general technique for giving a mind-blowing orgasm to a man with your mouth:

First, kiss his testicles lightly and then kiss his shaft and penis head. Let him hear or see you kissing his genitals, but keep the kissing sensation light.

Next, hold the penis shaft with one hand near the testicles. Run your tongue, with medium force, up and down the vein on his shaft. Then run your tongue all around the head of the penis.

Find the point of the penis under the head, where the penis shaft vein ends, and the penis head begins. There's a small flap of skin right there that is extremely sensitive. Take that skin between your lips and lightly suck on it and flick it with the tip of your tongue.

While your mouth is exploring his penis head and shaft, move your hand up and down the bottom part of his shaft. With a firm grip (remember, he's used to his own firm hand during masturbation) make an up and down movement, while your mouth pays attention to his penis head.

Take your other hand and caress his testicles. Pay close attention to your fingernails, so that not one scratch occurs in this tender area. It's best to use the back of your hand when carressing his testicles to avoid any chance of hurting him. While you're petting them, use your index finger to caress the skin between his testicles and his anus. This region of flesh is also extremely sensitive, and men love to have it stroked.

I know this is a lot of coordinating to accomplish simultaneously, but don't overly complicate the matter. It's not rocket science. The idea is to generate a lot of pleasurable activity in his genitals. You've got three tools for giving stimulation: two hands and a mouth. You can even rub your breasts against his testicles, if you're pliable, making five tools.

Once he's completely aroused by this foreplay, it's time to begin the oral sex. There are two different methods to choose from or to alternate between. Neither is more "correct," although your partner may have preferences that he'll convey to you.

In the first method, you kneel next to his lap and grip your hands around his penis shaft. Some men may prefer lubrication under your hands. Either way, you're going to grip firmly and move your hands up and down at the same time in a steady, rhythmic motion. Try not to vary the rhythm, but you can speed up or slow down slightly as you go.

While your hands are masturbating his penis shaft, put your lips over your teeth, as though you're imitating a toothless person. You don't want any contact to occur between your teeth and his penis. Relax your mouth and throat and think about how much of a turn-on it is to give your man pleasure. Don't allow any negative thoughts to enter your mind.

Put your mouth over his penis head and grip it tightly with your lips (still covering your teeth). Move your head up and down concurrently with your hands. Keep the rhythm steady, and your man will have an orgasm in almost no time. If you want to create a buildup of passion, slow the rhythm down. If you want to create an explosive orgasm, speed it up.

The odd thing about rhythm is that if you vary it too much, he'll lose his concentration and won't have an orgasm. But if you keep the rhythm too steady, his penis will become numbed and he won't feel the sensation keenly enough to have an orgasm. So, vary the rhythm somewhat—but not too much.

In the second method, only use one hand on the penis shaft. Follow your hand up and down the penis with your mouth, as you did in the first method. The difference is that you'll be playing with his testicles with the other hand. Also, your mouth will be going deeper down on the penis shaft.

An actress who earned the name "Deep Throat" because of her famous porn roles, in which she'd perform oral sex on well-endowed men, once gave an interview about her techniques. The Deep Throat movies, if you haven't seen them, are about a woman who has a clitoris in her throat instead of in the usual place. To have an orgasm, she has to have oral sex with men.

Her secret to success in bypassing the gag reflex when having a penis extend deep down her throat is similar to the methods used by sword-swallowers, the actress said. She explained that you have to concentrate on completely relaxing the throat muscles. If you tilt your head back and relax your muscles, it opens your throat up very widely.

Men love oral sex, as explained in Chapter Two. It is a symbolic act that signifies your love and devotion. It also feels good, and the thought of oral sex is a real turn-on for most men.

Oral Sex For Her

Most women enjoy receiving oral sex, although they tend to be more self-conscious about the experience than men. Women have been conditioned to feel that their genitals are dirty or foul-smelling. If you're worried about offending your partner, you won't be able to relax and have an orgasm. You'll be too uptight (remember the sympathetic nervous system) and you won't be able to concentrate on the pleasurable feelings.

Men who have tried performing oral sex on a woman may feel frustrated because the experience didn't yield a successful response. You tried your hardest until your tongue felt it would fall off, and she still wouldn't come. So you quit trying.

Here are some techniques that work well in performing oral sex on a woman. Although each woman is different, this is a pretty universal method that should make a woman have an orgasm. If you can make her come, she'll be very happy! Since it's a rare man who can bring a woman to a powerful orgasm, she'll never forget it if you master this technique:

First, help her relax. This is of integral importance, because if she's uptight, she won't come—no matter what you do. An interesting study printed in the *New England Journal of Medicine* compared common sexual difficulties of men and women. Forty-seven percent of the women claimed that their biggest sexual problem was an "inability to relax," compared to only 12 percent of the men surveyed. That's a big difference! There are a few things you can do to help your woman relax:

1. You can say gently, "Relax, I want you to completely forget about everything. Just let me enjoy giving you pleasure." Give her permission to receive pleasure. Women have been so socialized to be givers that it's difficult for them solely to receive without simultaneously giving back.

2. Tell her how much you enjoy giving her oral sex. If she thinks you're getting pleasure out of the process, she won't worry about being selfish.

3. Compliment her on her genitals. Reassure her that you love the way she smells, tastes, and looks. Again, this is a significant area of concern for women.

4. For an extreme way to ensure her relaxation, you can tie her hands and legs to the bedposts. Don't make this a threatening situation that will elicit fear. Instead, use beautiful scarves or suit ties and loosely tie her in a spread-eagle fashion. If she believes she has no choice but to succumb to your pleasures, she'll give in to the feelings more easily.

Next, kiss her gently on her breasts, stomach, and the insides of her thighs. Run your fingers gently in a circle around her inner thighs and circling around her genitals. Keep running your fingers in a smaller and smaller circle until you're touching her labia lips.

Take the lips between your thumb, forefinger, and index finger and rub the lips firmly together in a circling motion. Caress the length of the lips as you firmly continue to press them together.

Keep talking to her as you're doing this, reassuring her and helping her to let go and to relax. Keep your voice firm and controlled (so she feels safe), but at the same time choose gentle, loving words. An example would be to say, "I love to kiss you right here" in a firm but quiet voice.

Avoid saying anything that may make her feel self-conscious, such as, "I love to look at your face while you're having an orgasm." She'll be very embarrassed if you tell her you're watching her face while she's coming. This feeling may prohibit future orgasms, because she'll worry about looking foolish while you're watching her.

Spread her labia lips apart and go to the top where the two lips meet. This area is the clitoris. Even though women have nerve endings inside their vagina that yield pleasure during intercourse, it's her clitoris that creates orgasms.

The clitoris is almost identical to a penis, only it is much smaller. It is housed in a protective sack, from which the clitoris arises when the woman is sexually aroused. There's even a little "head" at the top.

Hold back her labia lips to expose the clitoris area and flick your tongue very firmly back and forth across the clitoris. When the clitoris becomes erect, take it into your mouth and begin sucking on it. As you suck on it, flick your tongue very fast across it at the same time. This simultaneous motion will take practice, but it's worth it.

Once you master this technique, she'll experience incredibly powerful orgasms very quickly. Her whole body will buck underneath you. As she's coming, try to keep your mouth fixed on her clitoris. She'll have a longer orgasm this way, and probably will have multiple orgasms if you continue the sucking and tongue-flicking action.

Don't be surprised if you get requests for oral sex. The special orgasms this technique yields are very addictive, and she'll be hooked on you!

His and Her Masturbation

Mutual masturbation has become the safe-sex alternative for the '90s. It is a pleasurable alternative to risking one's life engaging in unsafe sex. In an uncommitted or non-monogamous relationship, the couple can share sexual pleasure by either masturbating side by side or by masturbating each other.

Couples in long-term committed relationships can also enjoy the pleasures of mutual masturbation. That is, once they overcome the stigmas and strong negative emotions connected to the topic of masturbation.

Most of us grew up with spoken or unspoken negative messages about masturbation. Some parental injunctions are threatening: "You'll grow hair on your palms!" or, "You'll get acne!" Some children are taught guilt connected to religious beliefs. Many boys had the awful experience of having a parent "catch" them masturbating.

It's no wonder that, as adults, we continue to carry these negative feelings about masturbation. Of course, we know it's normal to masturbate. At an early age, boys discover the pleasurable sensations of touching their penises. Girls usually take longer to learn about their clitorises, although it's a common experience for females to have an orgasm or to feel strong sexual pleasure while riding a horse or a bicycle. It's just that girls don't realize, until adolescence or early adulthood, that they can continue these sexual sensations with manual stimulation.

There are a couple of "truisms" disguised as jokes about masturbation. One is: "Ninety-five percent of men admitted to masturbating on a regular basis, and the rest are liars." In other words, all men—with few exceptions—masturbate. And, I would say, the vast majority of women masturbate, as well. Of course, no one can verify this information. But, those of us who are therapists or doctors, who are privy to a lot of personal information, are fairly certain that masturbation is a normal activity for most people.

For many people, the realization that their partner masturbates is a rude shock. They take it personally. "I'm not sexy or satisfying enough!" is the fear accompanying this realization. Sometimes men feel competitive with their wives' vibrators. Often, women feel angry that their husbands look at "girlie" magazines while masturbating. Yet, these are normal activities and the spouse's feelings are equally normal reactions.

If a couple can get past all these defenses and inhibitions, they can enjoy masturbating side by side. It's very arousing to hear or to watch your partner have an orgasm. Very often, this will inspire you to have an orgasm of your own. Alternatively, take turns masturbating each other (it's difficult to simultaneously masturbate each other, because of having to divide your attention between your own pleasure and giving pleasure to your partner).

A study on the subjective feelings attached to orgasms revealed some interesting data. The male and female subjects of the study were asked to rate the intensity and the pleasure level of their orgasms in three different situations: during intercourse, while masturbating alone, and while masturbating with another person present.

Consistently, the subjects reported that their orgasms were most intense (strongest) while masturbating alone. But their orgasms were most pleasurable while masturbating with another person in the room. Isn't that interesting? The implications for a couple's pleasure is clear. If you both can get over any embarrassment or guilt attached to masturbating, you'll derive some very memorable orgasms masturbating together. I believe it will make you feel closer as a couple, as well.

Women who have never masturbated (and there are a few) can benefit by purchasing a muscle massager at any department store in the bathroom or small appliance section. This wand with a spinning circle at the tip is marketed as an aid in easing muscle soreness, so there shouldn't be much embarrassment in purchasing one. There's a wide variety of well-known brands, with prices ranging from 20 to over 100 dollars. Look for a massager that has more than one speed setting, as you may find a high speed is too intense or even painful on your clitoris.

After you purchase your massager, you can experiment with it by placing it around your labia lips and around or on top of your clitoris. Close your eyes, lie down, and relax. Allow your feelings of pleasure to guide you as you move the massager to the points that feel good.

Then, when you masturbate with your partner, you can either guide him to hold the massager on your favorite places, or you can masturbate next to him while he masturbates himself.

A Sexy Place

Where do you make love? I mean, *besides* your bedroom?

The catalyst for boredom in our sex lives is the location where the act occurs. If you're limiting yourself to the bed, you're missing an easy opportunity to spice up your sex life!

Okay, so you have kids running around the house and you don't want them to see Mommy and Daddy naked. Fine—then it's time to get creative. You can explore different locations within the master bedroom, such as the bathroom countertop, the bathtub, the shower (doing it standing while the water's on full force), the floor, and the triple-dresser top.

And when the children are safely away from the house, it's time to christen other areas of your living space. Try the stairs for a change of pace, or how about the sofa? The reclining chair is another ideal location for creative lovemaking. Allow the chair to recline all the way while you're making love—even if it tips over.

The back seat of the car is another romantic hideaway that many couples forsake after commitment or marriage. Even though it's cramped, it's still a fun place to revive a youthful, lovemaking spirit. One sexy married couple I know often drive their car to secluded spots off the main roads (they live in a safe town, by the way), where they enjoy a "quickie" in the back seat under a blanket. They report that the prospect of "getting caught" adds to the thrill of the sex. You can also pile into the car while it's parked in the garage. Put in a tape of the music you listened to while you were dating, and let the good times roll!

It's also fun to have sexual interactions (it doesn't have to be intercourse) outside of the house. In an elevator, you can squeeze, kiss, or lick between floors. At the office, you can have a private "conference." How about a public restroom? Use your imagination—and never limit yourself.

A final word about location: Avoid having arguments follow you into the bedroom. Postpone confrontation until the morning, or return to the living room until the problem is settled. In other words, keep your bedroom a sacred haven from negative emotions. If you pair the bedroom with fighting, it loses its sexy appeal.

Waking Up From Sleepwalking Sex

Just as the location of sex can become routine, so too can the act. As mentioned before, it's all too easy to treat sex as the equivalent of scratching an itch. It becomes unimaginative, routine, dull, boring, dead. The partners act like they're sleepwalking, and the heart and soul of sexual intercourse is removed.

In extreme cases, the woman loses all sense of pleasure connected to intercourse. The sex act is a "duty" to be completed as quickly as possible. Her sexual fulfillment comes later or the next day, when she masturbates alone. The man receives a little more pleasure, at least physically, because he ejaculates. But he does so by fantasizing about a woman who really, really wants him sexually.

It's as though the couple's bodies are there, but their minds are gone. They are not really involved in the moment. They are making love to strangers—they are living for the future. How sad—and yet, how normal.

This couple needs to wake up and rediscover the physical pleasures connected to a long-term relationship. You don't need a new love to find pleasure again. You do need to take risks with your partner, though.

Ideally, both partners will read this book and discuss the information candidly with each other. You might want to lay this book on the bed or on the night stand, and hope that your partner becomes intrigued enough to flip through it. Most people are interested in sex, so if the book is readily available, chances are your partner's curiosity will be picqued. Of course, there's always the chance that your partner will feel defensive. "Isn't our love life good enough for you anymore?" he might complain, or, "Do you want someone else all of a sudden?" she might wonder. If this happens, it's probably because your partner is bored with your sex life, as well. And your partner knows that you are also bored, and probably is nursing some vague fears of abandonment.

What's best and most healthy, then, is to get the whole subject out into the open. Neither of you is to blame. There doesn't need to be any attacks or accusations. None of that will help you get what you really want. The arguing is pointless and interferes with passion.

Instead, focus on the present and the future. Try out a new sexual position tonight—either one of your own, or one of those suggested in this book.

Passionate Positions

Here are a few tantalizing sexual positions you might enjoy. Just trying out something new is pleasurable in itself. You may decide on some variations on these positions that suit you even better. After all, some of these positions require agility or suitably matching heights and body shapes, so not all of them are for everyone. But have fun reading about them, at least. And try out at least one tonight, okay?

♥ **Woman Standing, Man Leaning Over.** The woman stands next to a high surface, such as a table, a counter, or the bed. The man enters her from behind, leaning over her.

♥ **Man and Woman Standing.** This is a face-to-face position. It works well in the shower, as long as there is a way for the woman to brace herself while the man engages in his thrusting actions.

♥ **The Pushup Thrust.** This is a variation of the standard missionary position. The man is in a stationary pushup position, with his arms locked and his body above the woman. The woman makes the movements by rocking back and forth underneath him. The result is a lot of sensation both on her clitoris and deep inside her vagina, and a suction is created around his penis. This position often results in mutual orgasms.

♥ **Woman On Top, Reversed.** The man is lying down and the woman is sitting on top of him, facing his feet. She sits up and down, and he helps her with his hands.

♥ **Woman Sitting, Man Standing.** The woman sits on the edge of a medium-high surface, such as a table or countertop. The man is standing, and enters her face-to-face.

♥ **Man on Top, Woman From Behind.** The woman is lying down, with a large pillow under her abdomen. The pillow props her up, and the man enters her from behind.

♥ **Getting Carried Away.** The man is standing in a semi-bent position, so that he has a lap, and he holds the woman up, facing him. She is in the air, buoyed up by his arms, his lap and the erect penis. He moves her up and down.

♥ **Side By Side.** The man and woman lie on their sides facing each other, and the man enters the woman. This may also be done with the man lying behind the woman and entering her from the rear ("spooning").

♥ **Legs Over the Shoulders.** The man is on top and the woman underneath, but her legs are propped over his shoulders. This allows for very deep penetration.

♥ **Criss-Cross.** The woman lies on her back and the man enters her from above. Then he turns his body so he is perpendicular to her, and their two bodies form an "X" shape.

♥ **The Lap-Sit.** The man sits on the floor on his knees. The woman sits, with her back to the man, on his erect penis. He holds her closely and moves her in a thrusting action. He can stimulate her clitoris with one hand for an especially tantalizing effect.

The Magic Kiss

Probably the most sexy part of our bodies, aside from our brains and our genitals, is the mouth. I can't emphasize this enough. *Remember to kiss your partner during sex.* This is the single most important act that will revive passion in your relationship.

Kissing is romantic and powerful. Remember how the prince woke up Sleeping Beauty with one kiss? During intercourse, lock your lips together. In fact, here is a scenario for absolutely romantic, passionate sex:

The woman and the man are lying naked side by side, kissing passionately. The man is gently caressing her genitals with one hand and running his finger around her nipples with the other. She is running one hand lightly up and down his spine and the sides of his back. The other hand is gripping his penis and rubbing his testicles and his penis head. Occasionally, she puts both hands around his shaft and squeezes gently, but firmly. Their lips hungrily explore each other's mouths.

When they both feel like they'll explode unless intercourse takes place, the man gently rolls on top of the woman. His feet and toes lock with her feet and toes. They hold hands tightly. Their lips are continuously locked in a deeply passionate kiss.

He is inside her now. Deep inside. His thrusts are such that he stays deep in her, not moving his body far from hers ever. She puts her right hand on his testicles, cupping them gently. Their other hands remain locked, as do their genitals, feet and lips. He is deep in her, moving with her, moving together.

The man whispers sweet compliments now and then, spontaneous exclamations about how good the whole thing feels. How much he loves her. How he can't believe how great it is to make love with her. She replies breathlessly that he's great, that he feels so huge and stiff. So good.

He explodes inside her with a moan emanating from deep inside his chest. The meaning is clear: He's overwhelmed with passion and pleasure. He feels relieved, drained, in love. She feels reassured, loved, and pleasured. He rests briefly, continuing to hold her in his arms and to kiss her.

While he kisses her, he rubs her clitoris with his right hand. He whispers more sweet phrases that relax her and carry her to the point where her orgasm meets his hand's motions. They're both satisfied because their sex is romantic and passionate—and thoughtful of each other's pleasure.

Chapter Thirteen
Using Sexual Fantasy For Mutual Enjoyment

"When my husband and I are making love, I'll sometimes imagine he's the hero of the latest novel I'm reading. I feel guilty in a way, like I'm cheating on him. But, through fantasies, I'm able to stay turned on, so we both enjoy the sex a lot more."—36-year-old married woman

ᶠantasies are important to sexual satisfaction, because our thoughts guide the sensations leading to orgasm. Sexual fantasies take many forms:

♥ Imagining that you and your real-life lover are making love in a different setting, such as on a beach or a grassy knoll.

♥ Imagining that you and your real-life lover are in a sexy situation; for example, pretending that you're strangers who just met and were driven crazy with lust for each other.

♥ Imagining that your real-life lover is different than in real life; for example, a woman might fantasize her husband is expressing undying love for her and a man might imagine his wife is giving him oral sex.

♥ Imagining that you are making love to someone you know or have seen.

♥ Imagining that you are making love to a fantasy figure, such as a movie star or a character from a novel.

♥ Imagining that you are a different person; for instance, an admired movie star.

♥ Imagining that you and your lover are engaged in sex with one or more additional people; for example, imagining that a second woman has joined your lovemaking session.

Sometimes fantasies are kept private. Some partners openly share their fantasies with each other. Other couples act out their fantasies and dress the parts of their characters, or actually attempt to make the fantasy a real experience.

In this chapter, we'll explore the use of fantasy for mutual satisfaction. We'll see how men's and women's fantasy contents differ, and how they can complement one another. And we'll discuss how fantasies, if used in a healthy way, can bring a couple closer together.

"Take /\e!": A Woman's Fantasy Life

A common theme in women's sexual and romantic fantasies is a desire to be taken. That is, she imagines being swept up in the arms of her strong, handsome hero. He wants her so much, and expresses his passion so well, that she is overcome and helpless to resist his desires.

In classic novels like *Wuthering Heights* and *Gone With the Wind*, as well as in contemporary romance books, these scenes are often referred to as "bodice ripping." In other words, the hero tears the dress off the woman—not out of anger or violence—but because he is consumed with longing for this woman. He and she both lose control.

What about the so-called "rape fantasy" that many women supposedly have? Rape, of course, is a horrible crime that has nothing to do with sex, and everything to do with a man's hatred toward women and his need to control and to humiliate them. Yet many fantasies described by women could be loosely described as having elements remotely similar to a rape.

These "rape fantasies" do not involve violence or anger, and so are quite unlike the crime of rape. Instead, the fantasies revolve around the man taking charge of the sexual setting. He is the strong figure, almost a "Daddy," because of the role he plays as someone in charge and in control. He acts out of passion and overwhelming love and desire—so again, he is quite unlike an actual rapist, whose motives are hatred and twisted logic.

Because rape is such a hideous crime, I prefer to call this phenomenon a "Being Taken Fantasy." When you are "taken," you receive pleasure on two counts:

1. The man is expressing how much he wants you. Because he has lost all power to control his passion, he is exhibiting the ultimate show of how special you are to him. You are the most wonderful, beautiful woman in the world and he can't help but be overwhelmed with sexual desire for you.

2. Because the man has overpowered you, there is no decision whether or not to have sex. This removes all social stigmas connected to "good girls aren't sexual." You can be the Virgin and the Whore, the innocent girl and the naughty girl, simultaneously.

Sophia's favorite sexual fantasy has the "Being Taken" theme. She conjures up this fantasy during sex with her husband, as well as when she's masturbating by herself. Sophia says this fantasy always results in an orgasm:

> During this fantasy, I'm still the same person except I have this really beautiful body. My breasts are perfect, probably around a C or a D cup, and they stick out perfectly, with no sagging. My butt is also perfect, and I'm really toned, with no fat or anything.
>
> I imagine I'm a stripper in a really high-class place. I'm the top-billed dancer, and everyone in the audience can't wait until I begin dancing. My costume is a beautiful gold bikini with sparkles, sequins, and white diamonds sewn on. I'm wearing a white feathered headband, and four-inch gold high-heels.
>
> I use a beautiful long white feather boa to tease the audience while I'm stripping to the beat of the music. All eyes are on me, and the men's jaws are open because they can't believe how beautiful I am. The men all want me, and they're begging me, "Take it off!"
>
> I slowly unfasten my bikini top, and hide my breasts behind the feather boa. The top drops to the floor, so everyone realizes my breasts are exposed. I move the feathers around and around, still covering my nipples. Then slowly, slowly I let the boa drop to the floor and

there I am. I'm topless in front of the cheering audience.

The men in the front row stand to get a better look at my breasts. One man can't help himself, he's so overcome with desire for me. He comes over, as if he's hypnotized by me, and he reaches a hand up in the air, as if to touch my nipples. I like this man's looks, so I dance over toward him. He reaches up and grabs one of my my breasts and begins to caress it.

All of a sudden, it's just this man and me. He's gentle but insistent in his desire for me. He lays me down on the stage and kisses my breasts. I'm so turned on I'm ready to explode, and he finally takes off my panties and brings me to an orgasm with his tongue. I try to get up because I remember the audience is watching us, but he holds me down and enters me.

The audience is clapping as this man thrusts deep inside of me, holding my breasts as he climaxes with a loud groan.

Sophia's fantasy holds elements that many women find appealing. First, she imagines how much men appreciate and desire her. Women strongly want a man's sexual appreciation. She wants to be desired, to be acknowledged as "special."

The audience in her fantasy applaud her as the most beautiful woman in the world, which is an outgrowth of women's desire to be uncritically appreciated. It's a little like the girl who brings home a report card with an "A minus" and her father says, "Why didn't you get an A plus?" The fantasy for a woman is to be appreciated exactly as she is. If she feels criticized, she feels insecure that she might be abandoned for a more perfect woman. Or she feels angry that her man doesn't think she's great just as she is.

Sophia's fantasy involves being approached and taken by a man who loses control of his impulses. He is hypnotized by her beauty, and he must have her. Therefore, she is absolved of all responsibility for engaging in sex. Cunnilingus and intercourse are forced upon her, and she has no choice but to participate. Because the man of her fantasies is an ideal lover, she experiences intense pleasure and orgasm from his superb sexual performance. She is safe, because he is a good, loving man who is in charge of the situation.

The Return of the Knight: Men's Inner World

The theme of many male fantasies dovetails with a woman's image of being taken. He sees himself as a hero figure who is powerful and conquering. He is the Knight in Shining Armor *and* Conan the Barbarian—a perfect male specimen who saves the world and rescues (and makes love to) the damsel in distress. He is the clever sleuth who solves the murder mystery and who is rewarded by having his way with the beautiful mistress of the house. He is Tarzan, using animal magnetism on Jane. He is Superman carrying Lois Lane to a secret and sexy location.

Men's sexual fantasies are printed in magazines such as *Penthouse* and *Penthouse Forum*, and form the theme of XXX-rated movie "plots." Thirty-two-year-old David has a typical such fantasy:

> I'm at the video rental store, back where they keep the X-rated movies. I'm all alone, and this section of the store is separated from the rest by a curtain. I'm trying to decide which movie to rent, when the curtain is pulled back and in walks this gorgeous blonde. She's wearing a skin-tight minidress with high heels and no nylons. She looks at me and smiles. She looks young, maybe 20 or 21 years old. I notice she's not wearing any bra and her nipples are hard and sticking straight out in front of her large, full breasts. The dress is so tight, I'm guessing she doesn't have any underwear on, either.

She bends over to look at the videos on the bottom shelf, and her dress scoots up so I can see her pubic hair. She isn't wearing any underwear! I can't stop staring at her, and she turns around and sees me looking at her body. She smiles really wide and speaks to me: "Excuse me, could you tell me which of these movies is good to watch?"

She wants me to help her pick out a movie! I ask her what she wants to see, and she says, "Something really sexy." I have an idea, I tell her. Why don't I rent a few different titles, and we'll watch them together back at my place. "'You would really do that for me?" she asks with a smile. Sure, I tell her, not believing my incredible luck.

We go back to my place and put on a movie. She stares at the television, not believing her eyes. She tells me she's never watched an X-rated video before, but because she's a virgin, she wanted to find out more about sex by watching one. She asks me if I could teach her about sex. So, of course, I say yes.

I pull off her dress and she's standing naked in front of me. I'm ready to explode, but I want to take my time and enjoy this. I tell her to lie down on the couch. Then I undress and she stares really wide at my penis. I tell her to touch it and she runs her hands all around my penis and balls. "Can I kiss it?" she asks me.

I enter her slowly, since she's a virgin. She's so tight, I can barely get inside her, so I moisten her with some ointment I keep around. She's moaning and smiling, so I keep going until I'm all the way inside her.

I come so hard inside her that I practically pass out! She waits until I'm sitting up again, and then begs me for more.

David's fantasy involves more visual and sexual themes than are found in most women's fantasies. Since men are usually more visual than women, their sexual fantasies are more apt to center around an attractive member of the opposite sex, than are women's fantasies.

The man's sexual excitement is largely fueled by his attraction to the woman.

The ideal fantasy partner in many male fantasies is a young, gorgeous female who possesses the body of a sexually-mature woman (firm, full breasts, long legs, and tight buttocks) but who has the passive personality of a girl. She is appreciative and uncomplaining.

In this way, male and female fantasies share a mutual desire for an appreciative, uncritical sexual partner.

Many men's fantasies involve a woman approaching them, as the woman in David's fantasy made the first move by walking by him and speaking to him first. She made an innocent, non-aggressive opening remark, yet it left the door open for David to speak with her. Her inviting presence and her request for assistance reduced David's chance of rejection. She opened the door, and he walked through.

Men also fantasize about meeting an extraordinary woman in an ordinary setting, like the grocery store or the post office. The fantasy is much like David's. The woman is attractive, friendly, and approachable. She doesn't "come-on" aggressively to the man, but she invites a conversation that leads to more—later.

Intertwining Fantasies

Couples can enhance their sexual pleasure by using mutual fantasies. There are different ways to do this. Deborah and Gary, married 12 years, discuss a fantasy situation during foreplay and then silently fantasize during intercourse. "Maybe we'll pretend we're stranded on a deserted island," explains Deborah. "We don't like to talk much during sex, but it's a turn-on to know that we're both thinking about making love in the same fantasy."

Other couples, such as Marjorie and David, openly discuss their fantasies while engaging in sex. Either Marjorie or David will bring up a fantasy topic, and the other will "go with it." They have favorite fantasies they tend to use over and over, because of the mutual excitement it's sure to bring. They embellish the same stories with new details to keep the fantasies fresh.

Some couples even supply props or costumes to bring their fantasies to life. Greg and Helen, for example, enjoy fantasizing that Helen is a maid in a hotel. Greg is a hotel guest who is surprised when Helen enters the room for cleaning. You can probably imagine what happens next. For a realistic effect, Helen dresses in a seductive maid's uniform, while Greg dons a hotel bathrobe. Helen says, "We make the situation as real as possible, but we change it every time. Sometimes, I'll play an innocent—although coy—maid. Other times, I'll be a real vamp who seduces the hotel guest. We just change the story to fit our moods."

Since men tend to be visual and women auditory, they have different ways of engaging in sexual fantasies. To participate in your lover's fantasy world, you'll need to engage in his or her "language." This means that women can describe sexy visual images and talk about details that allow her partner to picture the fantasy in his mind's eye. It also helps if she dresses the part of the fantasy. Men can stimulate her fantasies by saying romantic phrases that make her feel wanted, needed, and appreciated. In that way, he becomes the romantic hero of her fantasies.

Couples should beware of inadvertently hurting each other's feelings with mutual fantasies. Julie and Ralph discovered this the hard way. They began fantasizing that they were making love with an attractive female co-worker of Julie's. Both partners found the thought of a threesome very sexy, and the fantasy fueled many deliciously powerful orgasms.

But after a while, Julie noticed that Ralph didn't seem aroused unless they brought the "fantasy woman" into their bedroom. "It was like we'd have to imagine making love with her before Ralph could get into our sex," Julie remembered. "So I naturally began to feel jealous, like Ralph wasn't turned on by the thought of just having sex with me. It really became a problem, because this fantasy was like a crutch. Ralph wouldn't come unless I described a sexy scene involving this woman. It finally got to the point where I'd see her at work and I'd be as jealous as if she were really sleeping with my husband."

Fortunately, Julie and Ralph had a relationship that allowed open, frank discussions about problems. They decided to keep their mutual fantasies limited to two-person scenarios.

Everyone fantasizes in one form or another during sex. Fantasy is a normal extension of childhood play. The adult versions of childhood fantasies take on more adult, sexually-oriented themes.

There is no need to feel threatened by your partner's fantasies. Like you, your partner enjoys fantasies that have little application to real life. For example, you might imagine yourself having romantic or sexual interactions with another person. Just because you fantasize about another person, however, doesn't mean that you want a relationship with that other person. There's a big difference between lusting over someone and wanting a full-fledged relationship with that person. A stranger, acquaintance, or co-worker might seem the ideal sexual partner because of his or her physical qualities. But could you really be happy with this person on a day-to-day basis, after the sexual novelty wears off?

Sometimes, women feel threatened when their partners read magazines like *Playboy* or *Penthouse*. I'm not talking about intellectual grudges against pornography; I mean, many women feel jealous of the beautiful, naked models on the magazine pages. These women fear being negatively compared to the models. But, strange as it may seem, I believe that girlie magazines are analogous to romance novels.

Men fantasize with their eyes. Women fantasize with their hearts. When men look at *Playboy* models, they are relishing images of "ideal" women. It's the same thing when women read romance novels: they are enjoying images of "ideal men." But since women get aroused by fairy tale-like stories of strong, paternal, loving, rich men, they need more than a mere photograph to engage in their fantasies. They need descriptions of his actions and his words.

I really believe that girlie magazines and romance novels provide identical escapes for men and women. Both *Playboy* and Harlequin make "mental extramarital affairs" possible. In the safety and privacy of your inner world, you can use the magazines and novels to create a passionate love affair that leaves no emotional scars.

"But magazines like that are so degrading to women!" is the common female protest. If that *really* is what someone believes, I certainly respect their position. But I wonder if some people are hiding jealousy or resentment behind their vigorous arguments that *Penthouse* demeans women. And if *Penthouse* is degrading, what about other magazines accenting women's beauty, like *Cosmopolitan*, *Shape*, or *Victoria's Secret* catalogues? Is it really a protest, or is it a defense against jealousy?

If men's magazines are guilty of portraying women as sex objects, then are romance novels guilty of trivializing men? Don't these novels equally reduce men to shallow characters and success objects? Aren't both the magazines and the novels guilty of portraying the opposite sex *as only good for what they can do for us—the readers?*

I think it is valuable to examine honestly our motives and opinions. As I stated before, I respect people who stand up for human rights. However, I don't hold as much respect for those who aren't honest about their true motivations. If you really come clean with yourself about jealousies (which we all have from time to time), then it frees you to hear your partner's fantasies without feeling threatened. You'll be able to separate a fantasy from a real threat. And you'll be able to share the deep level of emotional intimacy that accompanies honest sharing.

Mutual sexual fantasies are a risk, but a pleasurable risk well worth taking. Couples risk becoming vulnerable to each other by sharing their inner secrets about what arouses them. It is important to honor this information and not to misuse it. For example, never, *ever* threaten to tell others about your partner's fantasies, and never put the other person down for having a fantasy you consider kinky or abnormal. Your partner may never trust you again if you violate this confidence, so view the information as privileged—and as a valuable opportunity for the two of you to become closer.

Fantastic Fantasies To Try With Your Partner

Here are some fantasies you may enjoy sharing with your partner. In each fantasy, you both take on different roles and personas. Try different ways of engaging in these fantasies, from simply suggesting a scenario to fantasize about during sex, to acting out one of these fantasies—complete with costumes and props!

Photographer and Model

One partner is taking photographs of the other for a magazine like *Playboy, Playgirl,* or *Penthouse.* The magazine "spread" requires a lot of close-up shots and provocative poses. How will the photographer inspire the model to feel sexy and relaxed? Will the model's sultry nature distract the photographer from the tasks at hand?

Professor and Student

Oh, no! The student has a crush on the professor and is doing *everything* possible to get his or her attention. The suffering teacher is trying to remain professional while ignoring the student's seductive behavior. After all, students and professors aren't allowed to have sexual relations. Or, are they?

Repairman and Housewife

The dishwasher is broken and the housewife desperately needs the repairman's help. She's all alone in the house, wearing nothing but a flimsy bathrobe, and is not in a suitable position to be entertaining company. When the bathrobe falls open, the repairman must decide whether or not to allow his animal instincts to run wild or whether to maintain a professional decorum and fix that broken appliance.

Variation: Repairwoman and Man at Home

The man is in the shower when the repairwoman lets herself in the house. Imagine their mutual surprise when he steps out of the shower wearing nothing but a towel— or nothing at all!

The Rich Couple in the Limousine

Being chauffeured home from a wildly-expensive evening on the town, the well-dressed man and the gorgeous woman are sipping champagne in the back of a limo. The driver can see the couple is getting more and more relaxed, and the woman's skirt is hiked up dangerously high. The couple start to kiss, and their desire overwhelms them. They make wild, passionate love right there, in the limousine. The driver keeps driving, but can't help but smile.

The Pick-Up

What's your name? Do you come here often? The couple pretends to be meeting for the first time. There's an attraction so deep they can't help themselves. They head for the nearest private spot to make passionate love—hoping they don't get caught!

The Naughty School Girl in the Principal's Office

She's been a very bad girl, and now she has to pay the price. She sits in the principal's office and hears how he's going to punish her. Will he lift her skirt and spank her? Or just put her on his knee and give her a firm lecture?

The Doctor and the Patient

The patient is here for the annual examination, and the regular doctor is out of town. The new doctor will have to fill in and perform the complete physical. Since the doctor has never met this patient before, it needs to be an *especially* thorough examination.

Variation: The Nurse and the Patient

The patient is hospitalized and needs help taking a bath. The nurse undresses and bathes the patient, taking special care to wash well everywhere. The only problem is, the nurse's uniform becomes soaked with bath water. Oh well, might as well take the uniform off and join the patient in the bathtub!

The Director and the Actress

The ingenue actress is unsure of herself, and needs the director's assistance in her starring role in a sexy movie. The director decides the actress needs to relax and get into her character first. How does he help her achieve the true "essence" of this sexy role? What does he do to inspire realism in his actress?

The Wet T-Shirt Contest

She's a contestant on the stage, wearing nothing but a thin white T-shirt, a pair of skimpy denim shorts, and high heels. He's a judge in her wet T-shirt contest, with the perilous task of spraying water on the T-shirts and judging which contestant should win. What measures does he take to judge who should win? What lengths does she go to in order to get the judge's attention?

Variation: The Thong Contest

He's a contestant in a men's muscle-builder contest. She's a judge who has to examine each man from *every* angle.

The Topless Dancer and the Bar Patron

She's new to the profession, and unsure of what to do. The man in the front row notices the new dancer and wants to give her private dancing lessons. He goes out of his way to get her attention, and she responds accordingly.

The Seductively-Dressed Woman

She's at the grocery store wearing a very low-cut mini-dress, and she looks terrific. But she's so engaged in picking out produce that she doesn't notice that the male shopper next to her is quite struck with her. He's staring at her breasts and she catches his glance. He asks for help in picking out a ripe melon and she agrees to assist him in any way she can.

The Woman Without Panties

She's sitting across from him on the subway, bus, or train, wearing a short skirt and no underwear. She likes him and wants to give him a signal that she's interested.

But the train is terribly crowded and noisy. And there's only one way she's going to get his attention . . .

Strip Poker For Two

You are playing poker and one of you is losing badly. Off comes the shirt, closely followed by the pants. There's not much left to lose. What happens next?

The Mermaid and the Sea Captain

The captain has been adrift at sea for months without any female companionship. His longing for a woman is unbearable, and then he meets a mermaid. Is she a product of his imagination, or is she a real woman? How can he make sure?

The Harem Princess and the Sheik

The rich sheik is tired of his wives and wants a very special woman who can really please him. He decides on a virgin princess who is very beautiful. But before she'll agree to marry him, he must win her heart. What does he do to convince her to marry him?

The Undressing Woman and the Peeping Tom

She's alone in her apartment and has compete privacy to undress. Or does she? As she slowly and seductively slips off her dress, stockings, panties, and bra, there's someone watching her. He wants her badly, and must do something to contact her. And then what?

The Tour Guide and the Tourist

The tourist is new to this country and completely relies on the tour guide's help. Only the tour guide knows the geography and language of this mysterious setting. How will the tourist show his or her gratitude?

The Police Officer and the Jaywalker

The pedestrian breaks the law by jaywalking, and the police officer has no choice but to haul the jaywalker off to jail. Or, is there another choice? Can the jaywalker seek a lesser punishment? Is this called bribing an officer?

Chapter Fourteen
Happier Ever After

"Romance is something created in your mind. It doesn't matter whether it takes place working, in a car, or at dinner. What is necessary is the right tone of voice, good eye contact, and a relaxing atmosphere."—33-year-old married woman

The chapters you've read have focused on a prescription for putting romance, love, and passion back into your life. The material centered on what kinds of behavior, settings, and foods best contribute to romance.

Now, the key is to keep it up, isn't it?

After all, romance shouldn't be limited to Valentine's Day or an anniversary. Every day can offer passion and a variety of opportunities to express love. If you use your imagination, you'll think of fun, creative ways to communicate romance. Make a game of it with your partner, and you'll probably never grow bored with the relationship.

Make yourself this challenge: *Every day, I shall do one thing that expresses romance toward my partner.*

Then—do it!

Whether it's a loving phrase spontaneously blurted out, or a neck or foot massage, give your partner a love gift every day. Try cards, answering machine messages, oral sex, and great desserts. Use champagne, fire places, soft music, and cologne.

Whatever the tool, the result is the same. You create a love oasis that your partner will find irresistible. Your partner will want to be with you always—if you become a safe and thoughtful lover.

And, just as it's important to remember to make loving, positive gestures, it's even more important to avoid unloving behavior. Remember not to bring arguments into the bedroom. If you need to disagree with your partner, try to use a loving tone of voice. Avoid attacking words. And, of course, never use physical force to get your way.

The men and women surveyed for this book gave insight into the things that spoil romance. Take a moment to read some views about what turns off passion for many people:

A 42-year-old woman

A romantic mood is spoiled when things seem rehearsed. It's okay to plan an evening, but not down to every last detail. If things are left to take their own course, many times they are more romantic than if they are planned.

A 27-year-old man

What spoils my romantic mood is when a woman is too physical. I prefer gentleness between people.

A 34-year-old woman

I don't like it when a man is too pushy or moves too fast, when only his needs or wants are addressed.

A 25-year-old man

My biggest turnoff is when my girlfriend complains about the events that are happening in her life. I wish she had a more positive attitude.

A 40-year-old woman

I hate it when the man begins to discuss previous girlfriends or relationships.

A 42-year-old man

My biggest turnoffs are when the woman shows a lack of interest in me and there is little or no conversation. I also get turned off when we have no real common interests or if I sense that she is not interested in being with me.

A 30-year-old woman

What turns me off depends on the situation, on whether it's in public or in private. If we're in public, my biggest turnoff is when he pays attention to other women. If we're in private, I don't like it when he seems preoccupied. I guess the bottom line is I want us to focus on each other and make each other feel special.

A 37-year-old man

I don't like pretentiousness or self-centered thinking. I also don't like a woman to be critical of herself to the point of focusing on her faults rather than her attributes. Another turnoff is when a woman is out to impress me rather than being herself.

A 27-year-old woman

I'm turned off by unromantic sexual remarks. Especially if it shows that the man is only being romantic in order for his main objective [sex] to happen.

A 50-year-old man

Romance is spoiled for me when my wife and I begin to argue, or when she nags me about something.

A 31-year-old man

I hate it when my girlfriend acts selfish. When she's always wanting more after I've already given her everything I can.

Riding Into the Sunset

This list of people's turnoffs is not intended to leave you on a negative note. On the contrary, this list demonstrates that it is pretty simple to keep romance unspoiled.

Everyone wants the same things—common courtesy, polite attention, and companionship. No one wants to feel used or unwanted. If you strive to treat your partner with the courtesy you'd reserve for a dear friend, you'll go a long way toward keeping romance alive.

Our ideas about romance harken back to our earliest experiences with love. As children in our mothers' arms, we felt safe and unconditionally loved and protected. As adults, most of us search for this same feeling with a member of the opposite sex. You don't need to pretend to be your partner's Mommy or Daddy, but you can provide an atmosphere of safety and love.

The philosopher Ram Dass, author of *Be Here Now*, has said that romantic love is inside each one of us. We really don't need another person in order to tap into this feeling, but most of us are conditioned to think that we have to *be in love* in order to *feel love*.

According to Dass, the other person is simply a trigger that allows us to release the feelings we already have deep inside us. I believe he's right, because our feelings of romantic love are launched when we see a romantic movie or read a sentimental novel.

You don't need another person, or an ideal mate, in order to feel romantic. You can access these feelings inside yourself. You can express these feelings without being in a relationship, through writing, singing, or simply daydreaming. If you are in a relationship, you don't need to wait for the other person to make the first romantic step.

You can start the romance ball rolling. Remember, there is no rule book of love, no hard-and-fast rights or wrongs. *You* decide when and how you want to express love and romance.

I Love You, I Love Myself

With that in mind, you may want to begin your quest for romance with a little self-loving technique that I've successfully used with myself, with psychotherapy clients, and with workshop audiences across the country.

The use of affirmations, or self-affirming thoughts, is well documented as a tool for increasing positive self-esteem and cheerful emotions. There's really no magic to affirmations. Just as a sad movie, picture, or thought can trigger sad feelings, so can a happy movie, picture, or thought trigger positive emotions.

Affirmations are a way to increase your positive thoughts and thus to increase your positive feelings. Successful businesspeople and salespeople have already discovered the power of affirmations in motivating behavior leading to success. I've personally used affirmations to attain personal and professional goals including weight loss, television appearances, my education, and becoming a best-selling author. I've also used visualizations and affirmations in my love life.

To me, love and romance are the same as any other desires you may have in life. I made a mental picture of what kind of career I wanted, what kind of shape I wanted my body to be in, what kind of car I wanted, what kind of pet I wanted, and where I wanted to live. Once I visualized what I wanted, I then used affirmations to create a life to match my mental images. Affirmations simply gave me the confidence and stamina I needed to attain my goals.

In fact, I had my life pretty well situated, with a great career, good health, supportive friends, and a loving family, before I began working on creating the love life of my dreams. The first step, when I set out to achieve any goal, is to decide exactly what I want. I visualize every little detail, and then I write it all down. Once I decide what I want, the hardest part of achieving a goal is completed. Then, I keep this mental image in mind while I use affirmations to give myself confidence in striving for my goal.

When I began working on my love life, I pictured exactly what kind of man I wanted as my partner. I decided on an ideal height, physical stature, and hair and eye color. I knew I wanted a man who was gentle and calm, since I don't do well with temperamental or angry men. I knew I preferred a man who was a business owner or self employed, because I'm attracted to entrepreneurs, especially in creative fields. I decided where my ideal man would live. In other words, I filled in all the details. Then I wrote it all down.

As soon as I did this, I met Michael. And he matched every last detail on my list. It was amazing! And the greatest thing was, the attraction was mutual.

I shouldn't have been surprised. Every other part of my life has occurred when I decided what I wanted and wrote it down. My love life is not separate from my career life (in which I had long ago achieved success), but I had been acting as though my love and career lives belonged to two different people. I didn't expect success in love, and I hadn't achieved it.

Here are the affirmations I use for myself and my clients. I recommend recording these affirmations into a cassette tape and then listening to it for 30 days in a row. Your unconscious mind responds best to your own voice, even if you don't like listening to yourself. Not liking your voice is an indication that your self-esteem may be a bit low, and it shows that these affirmations may be especially needed!

When you first begin listening to affirmations, your negative thoughts will be triggered. You'll get automatic negative thinking, such as, "This is stupid," or, "I don't believe this," or, "These affirmations are crap." Don't let these negative thoughts interfere with listening to the entire tape, though. These intrusive, negative thoughts are exactly what keep your "love self-esteem" low, and they may be interfering with your achievievement of the romance and love you crave in your life.

Listen to your tape for 30 days and you'll begin to feel like a new person. You'll like yourself and your life better. You'll exude a confidence that is irresistible to others, and you'll find that you're attracting positive attention from other people. Self-confidence is the most powerful aphrodisiac there is. Remember the study we discussed about people being most attracted to relaxed, confident people?

Read each of these affirmations into a tape recorder at a slower than normal pace. Allow about 10 or 15 seconds of silence between each affirmation. That silent space is for you to mentally repeat each affirmation when you later listen to the tape. Enjoy!

♥ I deserve love

♥ I deserve the best that life has to offer

♥ I am a loving person and others are attracted to me

♥ I am a worthy person

♥ It's okay for me to be good to myself

♥ When I'm happy, others are happy, too

♥ It's okay to have fun and to enjoy life

♥ Today, I'm taking steps toward a happier life

♥ I am relaxed and confident

♥ I deserve a loving relationship

♥ My actions are motivated by love

♥ I deserve love for just being who I am

♥ I am a lovable person

♥ I treat others with kindness and expect the same in return

♥ I can honestly express my feelings of love

♥ I enjoy giving and receiving love

♥ I can laugh and have fun

♥ Today, I give myself permission to pursue my goals

♥ I take steps to give myself the life I want

♥ I deserve to achieve my goals

♥ Being good to myself helps others, too

♥ When I win, others win

♥ I deserve love in my life

♥ I surround myself with positive people

♥ I give myself credit for my success and good work

♥ I deserve romance and passion

♥ I expect my relationships to be loving and secure

♥ It is safe for me to love another person

♥ I can be open and honest with my lover

♥ It's okay to express love and appreciation

♥ I enjoy sexual pleasure

♥ I can accept praise and attention from others

♥ I deserve to be surrounded with love and approval

♥ I expect to have a good time

♥ I give myself permission to relax and to have a good time.

Reader Survey

To continue my research on love, passion, romance, and sex, it is necessary for me to hear from a wide range of people. I usually conduct surveys while traveling and while giving workshops, lectures, or during television appearances. You can help in the effort to track the research by taking a few moments to honestly answer the following questions. Since the questionnaire is anonymous, I hope you'll feel free to frankly and freely answer all the questions. Thank you, and happy loving!

Male _____ Female _____ Age _____
Marital Status: Married (How Long?)_____ Single_____
     Divorced _____
How many times have you been married?_____
How long did your last marriage last?   _____
How long have you lived apart?   _____
If you are single or divorced, are you now involved in
     a committed relationship?_____
Are you living with this person? _____
How long? _____
How often, during an average week, do you have
     sexual intercourse? _____
Do you have a favorite fantasy you think about during
     sex? _____
Please describe your fantasy: _____

_____

_____
_____
_____
_____
_____
_____

What is your favorite sexual position or technique?_____

_____

_____

_____

If you could tell all the members of the opposite sex
one thing they should know about your gender, what
would that one thing be? _____

_____

_____

_____

_____

Please complete this sentence: If I could change one
thing about my sex life, I would: _____

_____

_____

_____

_____

_____

_____

Please mail to:

> **Doreen Virtue, Ph.D.**
> **c/o National Press Books, Inc.**
> **7200 Wisconsin Avenue**
> **Bethesda, MD 20814**

Bibliography and Resources

Benkert, O. "Pharacological Experiments To Stimulate Human Sexual Behavior." *Psychopharacologia*, 26: 133.

Blum, I., *et al.* "Food Preferences, Body Weight, and Platelet-Poor Plasma Serotonin and Catecholamines." *American Journal of Clinical Nutrition*, Vol. 57: 486 - 489.

Blundell, J. E. and Hill, A. J., "Nutrition, Serotonin and Appetite: Case Study in the Evolution of a Scientific Idea." *Appetite*, 8: 183.

Blundell, J. E., "Serotonin and the Biology of Feeding." *American Journal of Clinical Nutrition*, 55: 155S - 159S.

Bowers, B.M., Jr., Van Woert, M., and Davis, L. "Sexual Behavior During L-DOPA Treatment For Parkinsonism." *American Journal of Psychiatry*, 12: 127.

Frank, E., Anderson, C. and Rubinstein, D., "Frequency of Sexual Dysfunction in 'Normal' Couples," *The New England Journal of Medicine*, 299: 111.

Gessa, G.L. and Tagliamonte, A., "Possible Role of Brain Serotonin and Dopamine in Controlling Male Sexual Behavior." *Advances in Biochemical Psychopharmacology*, Vol. 11, 217.

Jimerson, D. C., *et. al.*, "Eating Disorders and Depression: Is There A Serotonin Connection?" *Biol. Psychiatry*, 28: 443-54.

Jouvet, M. and Pujol, J. F., "Effects of Central Alterations of Serotoninergic Neurons Upon the Sleep-Waking Cycle." *Advances in Biochemical Psychopharacology*, 11: 199.

Koella, W. P., "Serotonin and Sleep." *Neuronal Serotonin*, Osborne, N. N. and Hamon, M., Editors. 1988: John Wiley & Sons, Ltd.

Leibowitz, S. F., "The Role of Serotonin in Eating Disorders." *Drugs*, Vol. 39, Suppl. 3: 33 - 48.

Malmnas, C. O., "Monomine Precursors and Copulatory Behavior in the Male Rat," *Acta Physiologica Scandinavica*, Supp. 395: 47 - 68.

Myerson, B. J., *et. al.*, "Monoamines and Female Sexual Behaviour,." *Psychophramacology, Sexual Disorders and Drug Abuse*, Ban, T. A., Editor. 1973: North Holland, Amsterdam, pp. 463 - 472.

Pennington, J. A. T. and Church, H. N., *Food Values of Portions Commonly Used*. New York: Harper & Row, 1985.

Renyi, L., "The Effect of Selective 5-Hydroxytryptamine Uptake Inhibitors On 5- Methoxy-N, N-Dimethyltryptamine-Induced Ejaculation In The Rat,." *British Journal of Pharmacology*, 87, 639 - 648.

Ramano, M., *et. al.*, "Effects of Aspartame and Carbohydrate Administration on Human and Rat Plasma Large Neutral Amino Acid Levels and Rat Brain Amino Acid and Monoamine Levels." *Am. Inst. of Nutrition*, 1989, 75 - 81.

Schuman, M., Gitlin, M. J. and Fairbanks, L. "Sweets, Chocolate and Atypical Depressive Traits,." *The Journal of Nervous and Mental Disease*, 175: 491.

Virtue, D. L., *The Chocoholic's Dream Diet*, New York: Bantam Books, 1991.

Virtue, D. L., *The Yo-Yo Syndrome Diet*, New York: Harper-Collins, 1990.

Wurtman, J. J., "Carbohydrate Craving: Relationship Between Carbohydrate Intake and Disorders of Mood." *Drugs*, Vol. 39, Suppl. 3: 49 - 52.

Wurtman, J. J. *et. al.* "Fenfluramine Suppresses Snack Intake Among Carbohydrate Cravers But Not Among Non-Carbohydrate Cravers." *International Journal of Eating Disorders*, 6: 687.

Wurtman, R. J., "Effects of Their Nutrient Precursors on the Synthesis and Release of Serotonin, the Catecholamines, and Acetylcholine: Implications for Behavioral Disorders." *Clinical Neuropharmacology*, Vol 11, Suppl. 1: S187.

Wyatt, R. J., *et. al.*, "Ventricular Fluid 5-Hydroxyindoleacetic Acid Concentrations During Human Sleep.," *Advances in Biochemical Psychopharmacology*, 11: 193.